Happy Kids

Understanding Childhood Depression and How to Nurture a Happy, Well-balanced Child

ALEXANDRA MASSEY

First published in Great Britain in 2007 by
Virgin Books Ltd
Thames Wharf Studios
Rainville Road
London
W6 9HA

ISBN 978 07535 12610

Contents

This book is dedicated to Greg and Jude,
my two most adorable sons.

☙ FOREWORD BY DR ANDREW MCCULLOCH, CHIEF EXECUTIVE, MENTAL HEALTH FOUNDATION

As a society we face a rising tide of mental health problems in our children and young people. This has been going on for at least thirty years and is set to continue. Whilst we in the mental health community have a fairly good understanding both of the roots of mental health problems and their treatment in individuals, we do not really know why this 'epidemic' of mental ill health in young people is happening.

But we can guess – it is, unfortunately, crystal clear that our young people are leading less mentally healthy lives. This is as a result of a whole range of changes in the way we live, many of which are alluded to in this book. They may include more sedentary lifestyles with less exercise, poorer diets, more target-driven education, materialism, and the breakdown of families and communities. In some cases, but certainly not all, we may also be talking about poorer parenting, whether this is *lasissez faire* or abusive, and drugs, alcohol and ill-considered teenage relationships.

We cannot stop society changing and some changes towards liberal attitudes have benefited those with mental illness. And our richer society is able to afford better treatment for all, including our children. But we have to tackle the iceberg of mental ill health in young people – especially as we know that this can be a precursor to and predictor of adult problems of many kinds.

Some of the response needs to come from politicians, the health service and voluntary organisations like mine. But it is parents who are in the front line in dealing with children's mental health problems including depression, the most common mental health problem worldwide. This excellent book gives hope and practical advice to parents on how they might help their child overcome his or her problems. Quite rightly it avoids simplistic explanations and treatment options but puts childhood distress in a family and holistic context. It offers a range of possible solutions including therapy, exercise and dietary change which parents may wish to use in combination and, where necessary, with appropriate medical or psychological advice.

There is much evidence that 'good enough' parenting protects children's mental health. Best of all, this book may help parents protect their children by offering them a more mentally healthy family life. Then we will all be winners.

🏠 FOREWORD BY DR STEPHEN TURBERVILLE, CONSULTANT CHILD AND ADOLESCENT PSYCHIATRIST

Most of us, whatever our age, feel low or down at times, but when we can't shake this feeling off and it starts to take over all aspects of our lives then we are probably depressed. The recognition over the past couple of decades that depression is an illness that affects not just adults, but children and adolesents too, has been a major step forward in addressing the emotional suffering of a significant number of young people.

No child or young person can be seen in isolation from the family or caregivers around them and equally the effects of depression are felt not just by the young person but by those who love and care for them too. Having a book such as *Happy Kids: Understanding Childhood Depression and How to Nurture a Happy, Well-balanced Child* available to parents in just such a position will be a valuable resource. What is particularly powerful is the fact that this book isn't written by a health professional or an academic expert, but by someone who has lived through the experience herself and struggled with the issues discussed. The result is a book full of useful discussion and advice for supporting young people and their families through depression and trying to address their long-term emotional wellbeing.

We all have a role in our society to ensure that we are addressing our children's emotional needs whether as parents, grandparents, teachers, health professionals, policy makers or wherever we find ourselves. The responsibility for nurturing happy, well-balanced children should be the responsibility of all and there is a message in this book for each of us. Clearly there is no single answer either to why children become depressed or one pathway for recovery, but I am sure that readers of this book will find not just helpful practical suggestions, but also much food for thought.

Introduction

🖐 DEPRESSION IN CHILDREN

Your children are not your children. They are the sons and daughters of Life's longing for itself... You may house their bodies but not their souls, for their souls dwell in the house of tomorrow, which you cannot visit, not even in your dreams.

Kahlil Gibran, philosopher

Happy kids are what we all want. As a parent, I am never more fulfilled than when my kids are happy. When a child is happy it can make the whole world feel at peace as they embody the quintessence of spirituality. They are entrenched in what the mystics have tried to teach us for thousands of years – living in the moment. They feel happy to be alive and enjoy the simple things in a way that is not only profound but is the only path to real happiness.

I have never met a parent who has set out to make their children *un*happy. No one I know has ever deliberately and consciously sabotaged their child's happiness. Most parents I know go through turmoil and angst to ensure their child's wellbeing. However, the figures on child mental health are demonstrating that more children are unhappy than ever before but no one organisation or authority on children's mental health can pinpoint the reason why. It's mystifying and worrying because these children are the next generation of adults who will lead the world into a new age. Helping our children feel happy now is the way to nurture a whole new generation.

It's really only since the 1980s that depression has been diagnosed in children; before that it was assumed that children didn't get depressed. The figures since then have soared. The Office of National Statistics (ONS) carried out research for the Department of Health, entitled 'Mental Health of Children and Adolescents in Great Britain, 1999', which stated that the number of children suffering mental health disorders in the UK was around 10 per cent, which is a staggering 1.2 million children at any one time. This has since been backed up by a further report by the ONS in 2004. Recent evidence compiled by the World Health Organization indicates that by the year 2020, childhood neuro-psychiatric disorders will rise proportionately by over 50 per cent, internationally, to become one of the five most common causes of morbidity, mortality and disability among children.

A parent's worry for a depressed child can leave everyone feeling fraught and anxious and will only make the situation more uneasy for the child. The help available to parents of depressed children is very limited. A study, entitled 'Growing Pains', of more than 400 parents of children aged 5 to 15 was commissioned by Norwich Union Healthcare as it launched a national initiative to help parents get the best support for their child's emotional and physical wellbeing. The results, published in October 2004, indicated that 58 per cent of parents of depressed kids would not know where to get help yet 21 per cent said that seeing their doctor would be a waste of time. Dr Doug Wright, clinical development manager at Norwich Union Healthcare, said: 'It's often the case that while children's services are available locally, parents don't know where to look for information and advice on what they can access in their area.'

Commenting on the findings, Dinah Morley, director of children's mental health charity YoungMinds says: 'The results of the "Growing Pains" study clearly show that mental health problems are rising amongst adolescents in the UK – many young people feel desperately anxious about how they are going to take their place in the adult world. As for why this is occurring, we can only point to a number of contemporary factors which impact on adolescents, undermining their plans for the future and setting goals which are virtually unattainable.' YoungMinds says one in five people who call their helpline are parents seeking advice about their children's depression.

But, although no one person, organisation or body can explain the phenomenal increase in childhood depression, our children have a different environment to the one we knew as kids. They are exposed to many, many pressures which we didn't have. We have an embedded drug/drink culture which is causing havoc throughout the police and NHS services (40 per cent of A&E admissions are alcohol-related), as well as major concern for parents. There is a heavy academic workload placed on children to achieve at any cost; and self-abuse, such as self-harming and anorexia, appears to be much more mainstream and even 'cool' amongst some school children.

We now face an alarming situation where the public at large is having less to do with children – indeed, more and more adults are owning up to crossing the street to avoid what looks like an aggressive situation with a group of youths even though they have no idea what the youths' motives might be. And, with pedophilia hitting our press daily, it can feel like there are child abusers on every street corner ready to pounce on our child and abduct them at any minute, even though the official figures of child harm, according to the Metropolitan Police, haven't significantly altered in the last fifty years.

When my father was an adolescent he lived in a working-class family, in a street full of other working-class families. All the kids had more or less the same toys, bikes etc. Their fathers all did more or less the same type of job and their mothers were usually at home. There was little distinction between him and his friends which made them all much less divided as a group. They would play together out in the street and if they were naughty (we are talking about kicking a ball into some else's garden!) Mrs So and So from across the road would tell their parents and they would all get told off. This evokes a safe and structured, equal society which was regulated by the adults and contained the children's behaviour.

This society does not exist today and the new society seems to be changing at such a fast rate that it is hard to know what is 'normal'. For example, children seem to be so much more aware of their world than previous generations; they are much more aware of their personal rights; relationships with parents are evolving into a much more equal status and information is so available that we refer to our children for answers to modern technology. Yet, for all this 'advancement' together with the fact that we, in the West, have never been more affluent, it seems that children are not as happy as they once were.

❦ HOW THIS BOOK CAN HELP

We all want our kids to be happy and having a child who seems unhappy can put us, as parents, into a spin, throwing recrimination at ourselves. 'What have I done? What have I said? What do I need to do now?' Self-blame can take over and this can lead us into a panic which can lead to such desperate measures as moving the child out of school or getting the child placed onto anti-depressants.

However, there is another way. Firstly, it's important to understand that children have the enormous ability, in comparison to adults, to change themselves in a relatively short period of time. Given the right external conditions, their capacity for emotional healing and growth is staggering. Whereas an adult may need years to get themselves from unhappy to happy, children take months or even weeks. I use the analogy of a protractor. If you start at the point of rotation, a change of only a few degrees can lead to huge discrepancies as the distance between the dispersed lines becomes greater. Equally, when the conditions are changed by a few degrees at source, the difference to the changes along the drawn line are marked. It doesn't always take a lot to change the child's conditions to give him the extra support and it can make all the difference to his happiness. It can be the difference of a few degrees, a little extra time and focus or a new channelling of a child's energy.

The reason for this is that children haven't had the time to pack on lots of behaviours to take them away from their true selves like adults have. Adults are armoured with defences to make them impenetrable and this is why some unhappy adults need *years* of counselling to unpack all their layers and get to the core of their unhappiness. Children don't have that armour and they can change and adapt much more quickly than we can. This does, however, also mean they are more vulnerable to outside influences and we have to protect them and teach them how to manage those influences so that they don't create too many ripples in their personal happiness.

Happy Kids takes a look at all the areas which disturb a child's happiness and offers suggestions to help the child back on his happy path. The book takes you through the reasons why children get depressed, what the symptoms are and how to nurture a child through to recovery. It is divided into four main chapters. It examines what depression is and encompasses a checklist in which you can decide if your child is depressed. It then looks at the causes of depression and explains what effects this has on the child. The next chapter encompasses the concept of 'the whole child' by offering ways to nurture the child through the depression from the inside out. This section is the 'soul' of the book and is meant to bring out the very heart of the child/parent relationship. The final part considers the whole family and what maybe occurring within it that may have impacted on the children and this has a more profound effect on the emotional health of the child than anything else.

In many cases there is an obvious reason as to why a child is depressed. This could be the loss of someone close to them which can only create enormous sadness and grief. It could be due to the loss of a pet, illness, moving to a new school, a parental spilt or something else that is sure to affect the child. In these cases we can understand why a child is depressed; depression is part of the grief process and a vital stage to go through in order to come out the other side towards acceptance and joy.

However, there are many parents who just don't know why their child is depressed. This book is intended to specifically help the parents of those children by explaining why the child may be feeling like this and offering ways to help the child towards recovery.

There are some parts of this book which are hard hitting and this may not be relevant to your child. But, it wouldn't be right to write a book about helping kids become happy and not include most of the causes of a child's unhappiness. It is also necessary to look at ways to help an extremely unhappy child who is 'acting out' his unhappiness through behaviours we don't like. This book approaches children's wellbeing like a half of a grapefruit; you have to turn the grapefruit in side out to get to the fleshy bit on the inside. Likewise, you have to get to the 'underbelly' of any difficulties in order to help the child resolve his problems and feel good about himself. This is what this book strives to do. Take what you like and leave the rest.

In many cases the information is relevant to all aged children but there is a definite distinction between how younger and older children should be treated and they are roughly divided into 'primary' school aged children and 'secondary' school aged children, or younger children and teenagers. There is a definite distinction between the two age groups which have a natural break at around eleven years old. Younger children, before they turn eleven, are much more contained in the home environment and they may 'act out' their bad feelings through moodiness, irritability and tantrums. Whereas, when the child turns eleven they become more exposed to the outside world i.e. secondary school, and this will influence how they 'act out' their bad feelings. They may turn to more destructive inclinations like drugs and alcohol, getting into trouble at school etc.

The knock-on effects of depression can be seen mainly in teenage groups because their behaviour often requires more urgent attention as it may appear more life threatening. However, the time spent with a child of any age who is depressed is vital to help them recover. Each child has his own developmental path and you, more than anyone else, will know what fits and what doesn't. And every child needs to know they are the centre of their parents' world.

Having an unhappy child can make any parent feel like a failure. It can seem like the end of the world but it's not. It's the beginning of a new world and amazing things can happen. Children are very resilient and they love more than anything to be successful in their own right. They can recover and they will become our teachers if we listen to them.

I have seen some astounding transformations in children who have been desperately unhappy. They can recover to be magnificent people in their own right, full of compassion and self value, ready to conquer the world with their huge potential. I have known families who have been transformed as a result of a child's recovery from depression because of the impact their recovery has had on the family as a whole.

The main condition children need is to be heard and accepted in that moment. It is also vital to have faith in the recovery process and trust that the child is going through it in his own way. Children are not born depressed; depression is a response to something that has happened to them. If we give the child the right tools, we can help them to go through the process and come out the other end. This book encompasses those tools; watch them grow and recover.

[For the purposes of simplicity, children are all referred to as 'he', but this may refer to male or female children. Also, the word 'parent' has been used throughout but this may apply to a carer, foster parent or relative who is raising a child.]

 # Chapter 1
What is
Depression?

✪DEFINING DEPRESSION

The deeper that sorrow carves into your being the more joy you can contain.

Kahlil Gibran, philosopher

The definition of 'depression' in the dictionary is to be 'low in mood' or 'downcast'. But this description of depression hardly scratches the surface of what it's really like to be depressed. Diagnosing depression in children can be tricky, partly because the symptoms of depression can be misplaced for childlike behaviour. Moodiness, anger fits, withdrawal, crying, sleeping a lot, tantrums etc. are commonplace in children and can be seen as 'normal' childlike behaviour. However, in some cases they may also be depressive symptoms. Added to this, children cannot verbalise their feelings in the same way that adults can and they may not know why they feel like that.

It can come as a big surprise to parents when a child is diagnosed as being depressed because they have not expressed themselves as feeling 'down' or 'sad'. In fact studies show that depressed children appear 'irritable' or 'moody' more than any other emotion even when they are feeling 'hopeless' and 'sad'.

Nonetheless, what is so *exciting* about children is their ability to make changes in the light of new experience. Children are fast learners and they don't need a lot of encouragement to feel better, unlike adults who've had years to perfect behaviours that fail to set them free when good choices come their way. Children can turn their emotional wellbeing around in double-quick time if the conditions are right for them to explore and grow. In trusting our children, they will tell us what they need as best they can with their limited thinking and vocabulary, and it is up to us to try to hear what they need and act on it.

Why do we get depressed?

The pain passes, but the beauty remains.
Pierre Auguste Renoir, painter

To understand why our children are behaving in the way they are, it is important to understand what depression actually is. Depression is a result of feelings being suppressed. The very word 'de-pressed' suggests that something is being pushed down. We are depressed because we have pushed down emotions that we cannot allow to come to the surface. We constantly experience a range of emotions and how we handle these emotions determines the level of our emotional health. If we feel angry but don't express it in a healthy way, we will either 'act it out' destructively or we will ignore it and push it down.

Anger

'Acting out' anger is commonplace. We see it everywhere – road rage, violence, bullying, fighting, sarcasm etc. This is aggressive anger and the depressed person feels like the whole world is against him; this type of anger leaves the owner feeling like a victim of the world and he has to fight back to stay ahead. He feels that a great disservice has happened to him and his anger is about serving justice.

'Ignored anger' is when we push the anger down and squeeze it in. This type of anger is passive anger. It is locked up and its owner feels useless, hopeless and has very, very low self-esteem. This anger leaves a person feeling more depressed than those who act out their anger because there is no escape from it. There is a myth about anger that if we ignore it, it will go away. But the reality is that if we have a feeling that persists and we deny it, it will manifest iteself in other indirect, usually more harmful ways and this includes being depressed.

Sorrow

Behind the depression is sorrow and if we feel sorrow but
don't let it out, we hold back the tears until they are too
pressed down. The amount of sorrow is a mirror image of
how much anger we have. People who carry rage are holding
back a huge source of pain and they are too afraid of letting
the pain out because they think if they start to cry they will
never stop. The irony is that we only ever get what we can
handle. In the past I have put aside a whole day to comfort
myself when I was very depressed and I knew I needed a day
to myself yet I only felt what I could handle. Even though I
cried for what seemed like *forever*, it was only about twenty
minutes and afterwards I felt so much better and was able to
function normally.

Denial

Denial is when we block ourselves from pain by ignoring
what's happening. It's a very necessary tool because it helps
us protect ourselves when we most need it. A child uses
it a lot if he comes from a family that is going through
some trauma and the child can't acknowledge it and blocks
knowledge of those things from his awareness. However,
denial distorts reality and if it is allowed to go on too long
it becomes a pattern of life, which will drive anyone into
a deep depression because the denial will have to become
stronger to cope with the growing pain. Denial is not
deliberate; no one says, 'I'll ignore this situation', rather it's
an automatic process of which the end desire is to protect
its owner. Within the grief process it's an important part
of healing because it gives the person time to adjust to the
shock of losing someone or something. But, like anger or
pain, its use is limited.

We all face adversity in our lives and how we respond to adversity is a direct response to the way we have been taught to react. When children are born they come with a ready-made toolkit on how to handle their emotions. As they grow older they will bend and become pliant to fit in with the family structure, not always saying how they feel and keeping things hidden from adults. We all do this, but to what extent depends on the family's ethos.

The Grief Process
Anger, pain and denial are all part of the 'grief process'. The grief process happens when we have lost something. This process is not easily acknowledged in our society, particularly the grief of experiences other than death. Yet grief is often an integral part of most life changes and experiences. Families who can acknowledge their grief and learn healthy ways to express their pain can then free their emotional energies to focus on life and the challenges ahead. There is no short cut to the end of this process and the depth to which you go through it relates to the significance of the loss. Below is an illustration of the Grief Process:

The loss we experience may be as minimal as losing our favourite pen:

Emotion:	Which is:
'Oh no, I can't have lost it!'	Shock and denial
'If I have lost it I will be so angry with myself because that was a special gift from my mother'	Anger and frustration
'I can't believe I have really lost it'	Sadness and pain
'Oh God, I'll never be able to replace it'	Depression
'Oh well, it's just a pen and I'll have to get a new one'	Acceptance
'I love my new pen!'	Joy

You get the general idea. We go through losses every day and, for emotional good health, it is important to recognise and acknowledge our losses. Of course for a huge loss, such as the death of someone we love, the emotions are extremely powerful and the process can last for a long time.

Children go through their own losses and they may not be obvious to a parent. It may be easy to dismiss their loss as insignificant but it might really, really matter to the child. How many times have I said to my small son something like 'Oh don't be silly it's only a party you'll be missing.' But, when I kneel down to his level and try to step into his world, I can recognise that missing a gathering of friends can feel like the end of the world to him and a day at Grandpa's is not going to overcome the importance of him feeling like one of the gang.

The most painful type of loss for a child is the loss of self-respect and dignity. Loss of dignity happens when you can no longer sustain others' misplaced anger and a child is more susceptible than anyone else. Not only does this engender feelings of worthlessness and hopelessness in a child, but unless the child is told otherwise they will blame themselves. Children are a natural sponge and, from a young age, they soak up what we tell them they are. Those small comments that we think are harmless may be ingested by a child whose self-esteem is rocky and taken on as criticism. Any form of bullying is a utensil for chipping away at the wholeness of the child and being yelled out by a stressed parent can be hard to deflect if you're feeling low.

Depressed children do not necessarily display the symptoms of depressed adults. Instead of seeming sad or 'down', depressed children may exhibit bad behaviour or 'tantrums', seem agitated, clingy or become compulsive about activities like electronic games or tidiness. It's for this reason that it can be hard to identify a child as depressed. Many of the common symptoms of depression may be interpreted as normal patterns of behaviour. There is also the obstacle of language because children don't express themselves as an adult would. For example, if you ask a depressed adult 'Do you think you are depressed?', you may get a rational response such as 'No', 'I might be…', 'Stop asking me questions' or any other such statement. But a child will usually respond with 'I don't know' because they are not as articulate about their feelings as adults. Some may argue that expressing feeling is a learned technique and not one that comes naturally. It can take time and a careful approach from an adult before a child is able to acknowledge his depression.

Symptom checklist

If you suspect that your child may be suffering from depression, you may find the following checklist useful. The key to understanding whether or not a child is depressed, according to the NHS, is if the first two symptoms and any other two of these symptoms persist for more than two weeks:

- Losing interest in activities once enjoyed
- Prolonged sadness
- Significant change in appetite
- Not able to focus on one thing for very long
- Disrupted sleep patterns
- Withdrawn and unable to describe feelings
- Reportedly behaving badly at school
- Flashes of anger at seemingly small things
- Physical agitation
- Unable to be alone
- Unable to sit still for very long
- Easily crying
- Showing signs of panic
- Not joining in things they once did
- Seems to have lost friends
- Unable to organise themselves
- Talking about how 'bad' or 'useless' they are
- Being nervous and jumpy
- Seemingly negative about life
- Stating 'no one likes me'
- Lack of energy
- Clingy
- Playing computer games excessively
- Self-harming
- Experiencing mood swings
- Drop in school performance
- Showing and describing fear
- Repeatedly complains of ailments e.g. bad tummy, headaches that seem to have no cause
- Complaining a lot

Although touched on, this list of symptoms does not fully explore aggressive and violent behaviour, behaviour that might be seen as challenging or destructive behaviour towards others such as bullying, threatening behaviour, stealing or vandalising. However, 'disaffected' behaviour could be a symptom of depression as depression is about buried anger as well as buried sadness.

The American National Institute of Health states that adolescents often 'act out', obscuring depression with aggression, elopement or antisocial acts. It is very, very easy to dismiss an aggressive child as one who deserves punishment – end of story. But there maybe another story behind the aggression and if we have any hope of helping these children who are simply seen as 'problems' then we have to try and get into their world, understand why they are 'acting out' and get to the core of their pain. And it *is* pain because anger masks pain. By addressing the anger, it will decrease; as it decreases you can address the hurt behind the anger.

This list is by no means conclusive but instinct tells us when things aren't right and this list may be good to get some clarity and to gather some evidence if you are seeking advice from a healthcare professional.

❤ MANAGING THE SYMPTOMS OF DEPRESSION

Bitter are the tears of a child: Sweeten them.
Deep are the thoughts of a child: Quiet them.
Sharp is the grief of a child: Take it from him.
Soft is the heart of a child: Do not harden it.

Pamela Gleconner, writer

As described in the previous section, there are many symptoms of depression to look for if you are checking the status of your child's wellbeing. Those symptoms are generally behaviour based, but they can be more or less

narrowed down into four main states of emotion. This
section will explain how you can manage these four states
of emotion. These are: sadness, withdrawal, anger and
denial.

These are all stages of the grief process that are perfectly
in line with having suffered a loss but somewhere the
process has got stuck and the child needs help to become
unstuck and continue moving through the process towards
acceptance and joy. Each stage is different and needs to be
handled differently and, as the child becomes unstuck from
that stage, he will move onto the next stage of the grief
process. This is normal. Roughly speaking, all the suggestions
work for all age groups and you could apply most of these
ideas to adults too.

The aim in all areas and stages is to give the child hope,
help him understand his feelings and help him to move out
of his depression and towards happiness. By helping him to
manage his symptoms, you are offering him the equivalent
of a softly lit, warm and comfortable room, which he can
come to believe is a safe place to express himself. No parent
can make a child recover from depression but what he or she
can do is create an environment in which the child can heal
himself.

Sadness

Dealing with a sad child can be heartbreaking. Or, it can
be very productive. A sad child is one who is in tune with
himself and his feelings. Don't dismiss his sadness and don't
rush him. It has to be there to balance out his experience.
There is a purpose to his sadness; it is there for a reason.
Sadness is a direct response to loss. What you can do is
become a safe place for him to share his sadness and to
express that loss. The loss maybe obvious, e.g. death of a pet,

but the sadness may be less obvious, e.g. loss of self-esteem through bullying.

Sometimes it doesn't matter what the loss is and you may get less response about *why* the child is sad, the younger the child is. What does matter is that you acknowledge the loss and the hurt.

How to help a sad child

Here are the foundation tools you will need to help your child to resolve his depression. These are fundamental in building a safe place in which the child can open up and explore his feelings. These tools are the fundamentals that counsellors use to help their clients through distress:

EMPATHY
OBJECTIVITY
MIRRORING
RESOLVING

Empathy

Empathy is feeling concern and understanding for another's situation or feelings. The way to become an empathetic parent is to become his best friend. To do that we must become a loving and safe person with whom the child can share his feelings and thoughts. This can be hard; we want to rush them, we want them to see that their sadness is unfounded. We want to show them that you can move into the future, the good stuff and not to take too much notice of an event. But we have had this experience and this child hasn't. We know what it's like to 'get over' something. A depressed child may not have an inkling that it's going to turn out OK and, if we push them faster than they are able to go, we will push away their willingness to talk to us because we won't feel safe to them.

And, when they do finally talk about what's wrong, we have to understand it as they understand it. We have to step out of our height and get down to our child's height. We have to see the world the way they see it. We have to feel their world and suspend our own belief on how the problem can be resolved. Indeed their problem may be resolved in an instant, e.g. they feel left out because they want to go to a party but the family has different plans – yes, that can be changed to accommodate the child's wishes but allow the child to go through his feelings first. It's not necessary to 'fix' them straight away but to express empathy for the child. It is an invaluable resource to be able to deeply share one's pain without judgement and this can lead to self-trust and self-belief, which will encourage a profound self-confidence in the child as he knows that his feelings are very, very important to us.

Objectivity

At the same time, when communicating with a child, it is important to stay objective. Having empathy and objectivity is the key to supporting a child through his sadness and this is the same for all ages. This is the central core of the way many therapists work. Whilst helping a child through their sadness it is helpful to the child if we keep ourselves one step away from our own agenda and sit in a neutral place which will allow us to see the child's pain without falling apart ourselves. Keep it *separate* and keep it *clear*. The child needs us to be whole and complete, hopeful, with answers, and strong enough that the information won't break us and stop us loving him.

If a child expresses hurt because of what we may have said to him, it can seem a natural reaction to jump in and say, 'No, no, that's not what I meant. What I meant was…' or 'Don't be silly you know I didn't mean it' etc. Hard as it may be, it's really helpful for the child if we stay unbiased whilst he shares his sadness and give him all the time he needs to get it all out.

Mirroring

Mirroring back what someone has said is another tool used by therapists, which corroborates what someone is saying. It is a brilliant tool to use with children. To mirror back, you repeat what the child has said in a way that they will understand and feel as if you have heard them. The mirroring must be as close to what the child has said as you can possibly get. If you can do it, *word for word* is best.

If you are not sure how to do this, practise with someone by repeating what he or she has said in a responsive manner. Try it with the next person you speak to – take one sentence and repeat it word for word. It's amazing how quickly people open up when you do this, as if they have been heard by someone else for the first time in their life! Mirroring is also an opportunity for the other person to put you right if you got what they're trying to say wrong. We do it all the time – we make assumptions about what other people think, have just said and what they meant. We are wrong most of the time too. So, by mirroring, we can concentrate on what the other person is saying and repeat it back to them. It's much harder than it sounds because the temptation to manipulate with our own slant is compelling.

Resolving

Resolving is offering solutions to help the child to move on. A child cannot always see the answers and we have to help him with our own wisdom. Our solution may not fit his situation and so we can offer another solution.

For example, my seven-year-old son was telling me how he was 'bullied' by Phillip at school. I asked him what, in his wildest dreams, would he like to say to Phillip and he said he wanted to kill him; when I asked how, he responded, 'by cutting him in half with a sword'. This exemplified to me how angry he was and I suggested that instead of carrying through his desire we should speak to the teacher about it and get her to speak to Phillip and ensure it doesn't happen again.

The solutions must fit our plan too so that we can carry out the suggestions. There is no point in trying to pacify a child with promises that won't work; they have got to be within our own limits.

Putting everything together

So, we can help our depressed child with empathy, objectivity, mirroring and resolving all at the same time. Two simple examples follow:

Parent: How was your first day back at school?
Child: I don't like school.
Parent: OK, so you don't like school. What is it about the school you don't like?
Child: I haven't got any friends.
Parent: You haven't got any friends. How do you feel about that?
Child: I feel sad.
Parent: So, you feel sad because you don't have any friends?
Child: Yes and I don't want to go there any more.
Parent: So you don't want to go back to school?
Child: Yes.
Parent: Well, that makes sense that you don't want to go back because you feel sad. But I know some other children who feel sad too because they haven't got any friends. Shall we

invite them round for tea and then you can be each other's
friend?
Child: OK.

In empathising, mirroring, staying objective and offering
a solution, the parent becomes a safe place for the child to
share their sadness and feel heard. The parent is confirming
the child's feelings, which will help the child to believe he
is OK. The parent then explains he is not isolated with his
feelings and other people feel the same way. Then, the parent
finds a way to build a bridge from his feelings of isolation to
feelings of being included.

For older children this is slightly different. Teenagers,
by their very nature are secretive and the last person they
may want to share with is their parent. But if the child is
depressed, their sadness needs to be addressed. It may be
easier to help your older child talk about their sadness if
you begin to talk about yourself. As kids get older they will
respond more to a parent being honest about their own
feelings rather than a full-on question time. The empathetic,
objective, mirroring approach still takes place but it is subtle.
An example follows:

Parent: I've been feeling completely stressed out today.
Child: Have you? Why?
Parent: Sometimes nothing comes right no matter how hard
I try.
Child: Yes, that happens with me too.
Parent: Then when I get stressed it seems to affect lots of
other things.
Child: Like what?
Parent: How I'm getting on with others or dealing with stuff
at work.
Child: Yes, I'm really hating school at the moment.

Parent: So you're feeling down about school?
Child: Yes. No matter what I do the others don't like me.
Parent: So you're feeling down because you think the others don't like you?
Child: Yeah and Sarah's not speaking to me at the moment.
Parent: So you're not friends with Sarah at the moment? How do you feel about it?
Child: Oh, I just feel left out and bad.
Parent: I know that feeling. I get that too sometimes. But for me, it does change if I give it a couple of days. Hey, let's go and get a good film for tonight, what do you say?

Obviously these are simple examples with two different approaches but by empathising, mirroring and being available for the child the result can be very powerful because in offering ourselves to the child in such a gentle way our greatest gifts are obtainable to the child.

A crucial element when supporting a depressed child is to remember that a few words go a long way. When Joshua (15) had stolen something and thought he was going to get found out, he felt suicidal. When he finally confessed to his mother and she said don't worry we will sort this out, it made the whole two weeks of terror and near suicidal action just sweep away. His mother could have said, 'You idiot, what have you been playing at?' and she would have lost him because he would never, ever have trusted her again. In the same light, if a younger child volunteers some information it is important for the parent not to make any judgement on the information but see past the action and inside the child with his fear and pain and his little eyebrows knitting together. If a child confesses to us, it's a gift and we have to accept it that way; a couple of soothing sentences and a loving embrace can take away all the panic in an instant.

Other ways to help an unhappy child

PHYSICAL COMFORT

We need four hugs a day for survival. We need eight hugs a day
for maintenance. We need twelve hugs a day for growth.

Virginia Satir, writer

Nothing feels more reassuring than a loving hug, a touch of
the cheek or a squeeze of the hand. We cannot underestimate
how powerful physical comfort is. It's easy to forget how much
we loved being hugged as children. We felt cherished and at
ease in the arms of a parent. A ruffle of the hair or a pinch of
the cheek can say more than words at those special times.

Some kids, however, don't want to be touched when
they are depressed. They may draw away from you if you
try to get close to them. They might shun an outstretched
arm or, if you do embrace them, they might feel rigid and
unbending. These children don't feel safe with physical touch
and we have to respect that. What has happened to affect
them this way we may have no idea but they are protecting
themselves and, until they feel safe, we will only be violating
them if we try to hug them.

But at the same time, they may be extremely clingy so you
have the feeling that they do need you but they don't need
physical comfort and that has to be OK.

LOADS OF REASSURANCE

If there is anything we wish to change in the child, we should first
examine it and see whether it is not something that could better
be changed in ourselves.

Carl Gustav Jung, psychologist

It's at this point that you can give the child loads of
reassurance. Children need to be reassured that their parents

have everything under control. They need to know that they are loved and cherished no matter how they feel. They need to believe us when we say we are 100 per cent behind them. They have to know we will be available at any time if they need to talk. It's important to maintain close contact with a depressed child and reassure them that we are right by their side. We need to reassure them that we will keep them safe.

WALK AND TALK

The work will wait while you show the child the rainbow, but the rainbow won't wait while you do the work.

Anonymous

Many studies have shown that exercising helps with mood and feeling happy. One study has shown that just thirty minutes of walking can actually give you a boost of good feelings straight away[1]. And, not only does the walking get you feeling better but it can also get you talking with your child.

Some children are much more open to talking about their problems if they are not looking directly at the parent. Taking a walk is an ideal opportunity for a child to be with a parent and gain the benefits of fresh air and sunlight, which boosts the mood, but also to be listened to. Walking and talking is very companionable and gives an opportunity to get along without any pressure.

---

1 Media release, University of Texas at Austin, 'Exercise boosts mood in depressed patients: study notes quick gains in vigour, well-being', 17 January 2006

PAINTING

Every time a child says, 'I don't believe in fairies,' there's a little fairy somewhere that falls down dead.

Peter Pan

Art therapy has long been considered useful in helping children to express themselves but it goes further than that. In 1999, a Sussex University study showed that art therapy can combat depression and some mental health providers turn to art therapy to help diagnose depressed patients.

In a smaller way, using the idea that art can help depressed children express themselves is something that can be easily done at home. Painting pictures is very relaxing in its own right, which then makes it possible to ask the child a couple of questions that he has been either unable or unwilling to answer.

Once the paint starts to flow it's amazing to see how expressive they become through their pictures. When you have a picture in front of you, you can apply the empathy, mirroring, objectivity concept and ask them all about their creation.

A simple example follows:

Parent: Can you tell me about your picture?
Child: It's a big dark cloud.
Parent: Yes, I can see that it's a big dark cloud. Is it scary or kind?
Child: No it's very scary – look at the lightning.
Parent: I can see the lightning – that must make a big noise.
Child: Yes and I have to jump under the bed.
Parent: You have to jump under the bed when you hear the lightning?
Child: Yes, because it scares me.

Parent: You jump under the bed when you hear the lightning because it scares you?
Child: Yes, just like when I hear you and Daddy arguing...

This is a theoretical conversation but I have had similar conversations with children and it can lead to them opening up about something other than the picture. It's important not to press the child as you may come to a halt but, in the child being able to express his depression in a picture, it could be the start of recovery. When my elder son was depressed I encouraged him to paint how his feelings felt at that moment. Sometimes they would be very black and dense but as time went on they became lighter in colour, more like a picture and less like a big dark blob. I made painting the first thing we did when we got back into the house after school and work and, because I got into a routine, it was no problem to get the paints out of the drawer and a couple of sheets of paper. I was able to get tea on the go while he painted and we chatted along the way.

Like with walking, painting also offers the child an opportunity to chat without feeling pressured and it goes especially well if the adult paints too!

Withdrawal

What happens when a child just won't communicate? They sit scrunched up with their arms folded around their body. If you try to talk to them they may seem disinterested in what you have to say. They pull away when you try to get close; they don't give anything away when you prod them with words. It's easy to become frustrated and angry at their lack of willingness to open up but your frustration will not come across as anything but critical. You know they are depressed and you desperately want to help but you can't seem to get through.

Ways to help a withdrawn child

The answer is just to be there, be available, be still and be consistent. Children are much more perceptive than we give them credit for. They haven't had the years of relentless knocks, like us, during which they've needed to armour themselves. Their sensitivity to our moods is uncannily accurate. The way we present ourselves to a child will affect whether or not they open up. Are we full of issues? If we are, the child will know it and may stay away for his own protection. Some children can grow a sixth sense that is tuned into adults' moods. They know when it's safe to come out of their shell and when it's not.

RIDING IN TANDEM

One great technique to try and approach a withdrawn child is to ride in tandem. Like taking a walk, riding in tandem means that you are undertaking some physical activity while talking to them. The activity takes the direct focus off them, which gives them a chance to breathe.

My teenage son and I have the best conversations while we are either in the car together or washing up. Because I'm on a mission (like trying to get a job done or concentrating on the roads), he is able to speak without me on his case with questions and directness. And, because I am busy, I am not capable of picking up every lilt of his sentence and analysing it! While riding in tandem, you can approach a withdrawn child with a gentle hand. Opening up with a statement about how you are doing may allow enough space for the child to respond with how he's feeling. It probably won't happen the first time. You may have to establish some kind of routine before he will start to confide in you. By doing the washing up, or some other activity, on a regular basis, you can create the right conditions for openness by being present in his company and not becoming affected by anything else. In time he will come to trust that activity as a time for sharing.

For younger children, it is necessary to become more a part of their world. So, instead of undertaking an adult activity with which to ride in tandem, you need to be doing what they're doing. Playing with them in their play world is a great way of building a trusting time for them to open up. Playing means actually getting in the Wendy house, doing the jigsaw or playing football. Primary school aged children love it when you join in their games – they have so much fun and it helps them feel included in your world. Once a routine is established, you can begin asking those delicate questions from which you may have been previously rebuffed.

Trying to encourage a child out of his shell can be so frustrating and, ironically, we have to overcome our frustration to become quiet and still, patient and understanding. Time will bring him out of himself and that will be in *his* own time, when he feels safe.

Anger

Anger is a difficult emotion to deal with at the best of times because angry people can seem very frightening. What is so brilliant about a child expressing anger is that they are so honest. They don't hold back and try to cover anything up like adults do. They say it how it is and – wow! That can be painful to take at times. But if the child is getting it out it means his depression will release. Suppressed anger equals depressed child.

What we can do is structure the environment for expressing anger. This means creating a safety net in order that expressing anger becomes a human right and is not seen as a violation. Of course the adults need to be prepared to hear the anger and that is not always easy but is dealt with in Chapter 4 'A Family Affair'. Remember, someone is more disposed to committing a crime in the absence of being able to express anger. This is especially true for children because they are more likely to act out their feelings rather than verbalise them. Kids who have nowhere to share their anger are more likely to commit violence (according to the United States Department of Health and Human Services) and often young people turn to violence because they do not see other ways to endure what they are feeling at that moment and they may not anticipate the repercussions of their violence.

Tips for helping a child who is becoming angry over everyday frustrations

✱ Listen to what the child is saying about his or her feelings and be willing to talk about any subject. Young people today are dealing with adult problems such as love, sex, relationships, failure and rejection. Unfortunately, their minds and bodies are simply not ready for these stresses. It's important to keep up to date with the issues that older children face so that you don't feel completely ignorant when they are talking about 'emos' or 'sui'! ('Emos' are teenagers who dress in a gothic style; 'sui' is short for suicide and the reason that it's shortened is so that teenagers can talk about suicide on web forums and not get banned because that word is not allowed on some sites.) You don't need to speak like a teenager but it's good to understand what they are talking about!

✱ Provide comfort and assurance. Tell the child that it's OK to feel angry and that angry feelings are important.

✱ Tell the child that everyone experiences anger. Tell him or her about the last time you felt really angry and how you dealt with that anger in a positive way. Explain in a way that's appropriate for the child's age and that demonstrates how anger can move mountains in a powerful and positive way!

✹ Teach basic problem-solving skills. When upsetting situations arise, the child who has practised these skills will be more likely to think through the consequences of different actions and will, ultimately, make a better choice than violence.

✹ Acknowledge good behaviour. When a child deals with his or her anger in a positive way, praise the positive choice. Take every opportunity to reinforce strengths. Build the child's awareness of his or her own talents and abilities.

✹ Finish by telling them about one great talent they have which you admire.

Of course if the child is abusive with his anger then this must be contained. It is unacceptable for a child to behave violently towards anyone else. Boundaries must be clearly drawn around the child who is out of control with his anger. It must be explained to him, when he is calm, what will happen to him if he behaves in that way again.

Out-of-control anger can be frightening but in one way, quiet anger can be worse because it can eat away at the child, tempting him to do something unforgivable to himself. We teach children how to deal with anger by the way we deal with it. In Chapter 4 'A Family Affair' we look at how we can address our own anger strategies.

Physical activity
While you are setting the parameters for the child to learn to best express his anger, it is worth getting him involved in some kind of physical activity because it is a brilliant way to help shift stuck anger. Not only does exercise

dissipate 'nervous energy', but it directly influences the relaxation response. A single aerobic workout 'burns off' stress hormones by directing them towards their intended metabolic functions rather than allowing them to linger in the body to undermine the integrity of vital organs and the immune system. Regular exercise actually decreases the level of stress hormones released during stressful responses such as anger. Thus, exercise can effectively be used as a preventive measure since it minimises or neutralises physical arousal to non-physical threats.

Exercise for primary-aged children

When you get the child involved in some physical exercise, it will work best if you become involved in the exercise with them. Depressed children lack self-motivation and self-confidence and it will help the child to rebuild some proficiency in these areas if the main parent shows as much enthusiasm for the child getting involved as the child himself. This will mean sitting by the side of the swimming pool, football pitch or dance class cheering them on or silently giving them confidence just by being there. After a while they may not want you there as they want to be immersed in their peer group. Team games are particularly beneficial as they can create an esteem that comes from being in a group that works well together. Choose your child's coach/teacher well; it can make all the difference. These activities don't need to cost anything as there are many community efforts run by parents across the country. Failing that you might negotiate a place for your child in return for helping out at the same time.

Exercise for secondary-aged children

Secondary school kids may not appreciate you being around as much even though their own confidence may be as depleted as a younger child. Finding a way to support an older child without seeming to encroach into his space can be a little more difficult but is achievable. Placing them in a class at the local recreation centre while you attend the gym or an exercise class not only allows them to feel that you are supporting them but also allows you to lead by example. Having said that, many kids do want their parents around but they don't want their parents to know that they feel like that. If this is your child, just ignore their complaints and turn up anyway. Depression may be as a result of severe fear of separation and you want to do whatever possible to avoid heightening this anxiety.

Denial

Denial; it's the path of least resistance. It's what we do when we can't believe the truth.

Anonymous

You may sense that your child is depressed but your child may not agree with you. Although he is emitting all the classic signs of depression his strenuous denials just shout you down.

Denial may seem from the outside like an ignorant state in which to live but it is a very practical way of keeping a problem at bay. Denial is a form of survival. Children who are denying their own depression need to be left alone until they are ready to come out of hiding on their own terms. Many unhelpful behaviours are self-created to assist the child to deny his problems. Although this may seem self-destructive, it has to be recognised that the behaviour is, conversely, a form of survival. It is about surviving the depression by burying the painful feelings and acting in a way that denies them. For some children, the reprimand over the unhelpful behaviour is not as great as the pain of depression but the behaviour helps keep the depression at bay. For example, a depressed child may steal and the stealing can create a 'high', which will take the child away from his pain. Drugs and alcohol are the obvious mood alterers. Now, eating excessive junk food can be seen as an addiction; I have certainly felt it myself – half a tub of expensive chocolate ice cream can change me from feeling lousy to feeling numbed out!

Medicating feelings is a way of the child not allowing himself to become overwhelmed with grief and pain. In many respects, that's worth a lot of respect and as a parent all you can do is be available for the time when the child stops using medicating behaviour to deny his depression and be ready to leap into action when the child asks for help. One of the hardest things to do is stand by and watch your child do things you know aren't good for him and there is a point over which you have little control. But, what you can do is be present and available for the depressed child, waiting for him to return to you when he is ready to come out of denial.

Signs that a child is in denial of his depression are apparent when you ask him how he feeling. Such a question will often solicit the responses: 'I'm fine' 'Nothing's wrong' 'Leave me alone'. Badgering a child will chase him away from you. Instead take the approach of being with him, playing with him, undertaking activities he enjoys and opening up about your own feelings. All of these can calm a tense situation and build a bridge. And, when you feel the time is right to ask again, two great openers are: 'What's troubling you?' (rather than 'What's wrong with you?') or 'I feel concerned about you and the effect that has on me is…'

Some children deny feeling sad; the only observable complaint will be of irritability, moodiness and boredom. As a result, they may get in fights or other trouble at school, interact less socially and lose friends. They may also 'act out' suicidal feelings, e.g. by cutting themselves, which can be misinterpreted by parents and teachers as manipulative rather than as a communication of distress.

All these things can worsen a depressed state. But, as a parent it is so easy to feel frustrated with the child who is obviously in distress but won't communicate. The overall approach is to nurture the child from the inside out (under Nurturing the Child) and if this means you almost have to rise above, or ignore, the distress because trying to get the child to see it your way is futile, then so be it. Every hour that you commit to cherish the child goes into the credit balance even if you can't see the balance sheet.

It can feel like sailing a ship when there is no land in sight. If you are an inexperienced sailor you have to keep going on instinct, trust and one or two technical tools, all the while believing you're headed in the right direction. Then one day, lo and behold, you see land and you know you're on your way home. The child will come out of his shell if his environment is steady and consistent because he will come to trust that it's a safe place in which to express himself.

Talk of suicide

The black moment is the moment when the real message of transformation is going to come. At the darkest moment comes the light.

Joseph Campbell, writer

This section is more relevant for adolescents than younger children. There is a marked difference between the symptoms of depression between primary and secondary school aged children. Very few studies have compared the symptoms of depression between depressed children and adolescents.

However, one study showed that depressed adolescents were more likely to exhibit suicidal tendencies than younger children.[2]

The NHS checklist for depressed children does not include thoughts of or attempts at suicide. But we cannot write a book about depressed children and not include this subject. As painful as it may be, the charity Depression Alliance estimates that each year there are around 19,000 suicide attempts by UK adolescents.

What to do if your child talks about committing suicide
If your child talks about feeling like committing suicide then stop and pay attention. Children, and particularly adolescents who suffer from depression, are at much greater risk of committing suicide than children without depression[3] so it's important not to dismiss talk of suicide as attention-seeking behaviour.

It is easy to believe that the suicidal thoughts or behaviour displayed by a child are trivial or are ploys to get attention. However, children's suicidal behaviour is rarely impulsive and their motives, particularly ones that are interpersonal, can be similar to those of adults. Some reasons why children may engage in suicidal behaviour are:

🌟 An attempt to regain control in their lives
🌟 Retaliation or revenge against real or perceived wrongs
🌟 Abuse from outside the home
🌟 Relief or escape from unbearable pain
🌟 They see themselves as the family scapegoat
🌟 To distract the family from other issues, e.g. divorce

2 'Clinical characteristics of depressive symptoms in children and adolescents with major depressive disorder', *Journal of Clinical Psychiatry*, 65: 12 (December 2004), 1654–9
3 *Depression and Suicide in Children and Adolescents*, A Report of The Surgeon General, US, 2006

:⁝ Acting out a covert or overt desire of the parent to be rid of the child

If your child has talked about suicide and you think it may be attention-seeking behaviour then they need your absolute attention. All suicide attempts must be treated as though the person has the intent to go through with the act. You cannot dismiss a suicide attempt as simply being an attention-gaining device. It is likely that the child has tried to gain attention and been unsuccessful and, therefore, this attention is needed. The attention that they get may well save their lives.

Here are some signs to watch for:

- The recent suicide or death of a close friend/relative, favourite pop star or film star etc.
- Preoccupation with suicidal themes
- Using drugs combined with depression
- Giving away prized possessions or making final arrangements
- Major changes in sleep patterns
- Sudden and extreme changes in eating habits/losing or gaining weight
- Withdrawal from friends/family
- Dropping out of group activities
- Personality changes such as nervousness, outbursts of anger, impulsive or reckless behaviour or apathy about appearance or health.
- Frequent irritability or unexplained crying
- Lingering expressions of unworthiness or failure
- Lack of interest in the future

By the time a child starts talking about suicide it can be a late sign in the progression towards a suicide attempt. **Take immediate action.** If your child indicates he/she is contemplating suicide, or if your gut instinct tells you they might hurt themselves, get help. **Do not leave your child alone**. Even if he denies 'meaning it', stay with him and talk to him. Ask him questions such as:

✳ Have you had thoughts of hurting yourself?
✳ Do you feel so badly that you have thoughts of dying?
✳ Do you wish you could run away or disappear?
✳ Do you wish you could go to sleep and not wake up?
✳ Do you have scary dreams about dying?

In response you can:

✳ Assure your child he can feel better, that suicidal thoughts are only temporary and that there are people who can help him
✳ Acknowledge the seriousness of his intentions
✳ Encourage him to talk further and if you feel that you cannot support him at that time, help him to find immediate help through your doctor
✳ If you've ever felt suicidal yourself now is a good time to talk about that period and to tell him why you didn't go through with it but how you felt like going through with it; this maybe the understanding and assurance the child needs

Talking to your children about suicide will not put thoughts into their head. In fact, all available evidence indicates that talking to your child lowers the risk of suicide. The message is, 'Suicide is not an option, help is available.'

Sometimes the family structure has not been able to support the child – for whatever reason – and the child needs more support than ever before. Make your own plan based on the child's request whether it be for the child to live elsewhere, the family to go through some family therapy, for the child to get hospitalised treatment etc. Something has made the child get to this point because no child is born with suicidal intentions. The reasons why the child feels this strongly maybe through no fault of the parents but for the moment all thoughts of accountability are irrelevant. The focus needs to be with the child and for the child. The child is asking for help and this is what he deserves to receive.

If necessary, drive your child to the hospital's A&E to ensure that he is in a safe environment until a psychiatric evaluation can be completed.

One suggestion is to ask your child's friends questions about your child. They may give hints that they are worried about their friend but be uncomfortable telling you directly. Be open. Ask the questions you couldn't ask your child or the questions he couldn't answer. Early intervention is the key to successful treatment for children who suffer from depressive illnesses.

The important thing to remember is that help is available, and there are plenty of useful resources and organisations listed at the end of this book.

Chapter 2
Cause and
Effect

One generation plants the trees; another gets the shade.

Chinese proverb

Cause and effect is the relationship between two things when one thing makes something else happen. For example, if we eat too much food and do not exercise, we gain weight. Eating food without exercising is the 'cause'; weight gain is the 'effect'. There may be multiple causes and multiple effects.

The first part of this chapter is to look at possible causes for the child's depression. The second part of this chapter is to look at the knock-on effects i.e. behaviours, of those causes. Please don't be alarmed by the Cause and Effect. While you may find reading this chapter distressing and slightly alarming, it's important to realise that by understanding the possible causes of your child's depression you can act positively and help tackle it. The effects are a direct consequence of the causes and so if you address the causes, the effects will diminish.

As I said before, children have a remarkable ability to change their mood in the light of new experience, and addressing the causes of their depression can have a massively positive effect on the way they're feeling.

😊 WHAT CAUSES DEPRESSION?

What causes a child to become depressed? There may be many reasons why a child is depressed and the causes of a child's depression may be very obvious. These might be the death of someone close to them, a parental split, a move to a new school, academic failure etc. If you can pinpoint the cause of a child's depression then you have a good idea on how to help the child through the process of recovery. You can console them through their sadness, understand their anger and help them to find a path through their confusion. Given this support they will naturally work through the grief cycle and eventually come to the final stage of acceptance and joy. Depression will be a part of that cycle but it is usually short and manageable.

However, many parents have no idea why a child is depressed and the problem is children cannot verbalise their feelings like we can. Depending on age, an answer to the question, 'Why are you depressed?' may elicit such answers as 'I don't know', 'I'm not depressed' or 'I just am'. Children cannot link their depression to events like us because they have not got the wisdom that comes with experience and the words to express their true feelings. Therefore we have to use a bit of guesswork, a bit of fact finding and instinct to determine the cause of the depression.

Children are not born depressed. Children are born with the healthy announcement 'I have arrived.' They have needs and when their needs have been met, they are happy. There isn't much more to it than that; that's how it is for everyone. But for children who are depressed something has happened in their short life that has emotionally tripped them up. For whatever reason, their needs haven't been met and they are disheartened and dejected.

Tip: Whenever you see your child, give him a big smile.

Criticism

Children need love, especially when they do not deserve it.
Harold Hulbert, psychologist

Criticism is a double-edged sword. We all need a little critical input sometimes. But if a child receives *constant* criticism they will do one of two things. They will either learn to mask their true selves by focusing inwardly with

self-anger and self-criticism or they will fight the criticism
by behaving destructively. Children can't make objective
judgements about the criticism and will usually take it upon
themselves that they are 'bad' and will then continually
act this out in a brazen manner. They believe that they are
going to be punished anyway so what does 'being good'
matter.

Studies[4] show that when parents frequently used 'intrusive
support', which is a term to describe criticism, children
become more vulnerable to self-criticism and depressive
symptoms. Children copy our behaviour and if we criticise
them in a negative way they learn to criticise themselves
which can set up a vicious cycle of self-destruction.

In April 2003, the Child and Adolescent Depression
Clinic of the Allan Memorial Institute site of the McGill
University Health Centre released the results of a study
at the Society for Research on Child Development which
confirmed that factors, such as negative self-thinking, play a
role in children's vulnerability to depression. Children, even
as young as six, are capable of developing clinically severe
depression if exposed to critical influences.

We may be criticising our children 'for their own good'
because we think they can do better or they're not achieving
their potential. But a child may be unable to live up to his
parents' expectations and before you know it, he thinks
that he is a failure and that he doesn't therefore deserve
his parents' love and respect. A feeling of 'self-contempt'
and worthlessness can overwhelm him to the point of self-
damaging behaviour.

When children get into self-damaging behaviour, they
hold themselves in contempt and behave accordingly. We

4 like E. Pometantz, 'Parent x child socialisation: implications for development
of depressive syndromes', *Journal of Family Psychology*, 15 (2001), 510–525

may think that their behaviour is illogical, but it is not. They have their own logic: 'I am worthless and stupid, worthless and stupid things deserve to be damaged, therefore I deserve to be damaged.' This is the logic of self-destructive behaviour. Their 'naughty' behaviour is their way of bringing about the punishment and destruction that they feel they deserve. A child's negative behaviour always has a hidden purpose underneath it.

Helping a child to recover has to include helping the child to criticise himself less. In order to do this the parent has to stop criticising him first. Parents may not realise they are critical because they may have received this same amount of criticism when they were children to no avail.

Once children begin to receive less criticism, two things will happen. Firstly, they will start to criticise themselves less, which will bolster their esteem and secondly, as a result, they may start to release some anger about how much criticism they have received. Depression is a symptom of buried anger and the anger has to be released to recover from depression. To effectively manage and cope with the child's anger as a result of self-criticism, and the misbehaviour associated with it, you must be able to understand the underlying reasons for it.

Tip: Give your child a big hug every day.

Neglect

Neglect is the persistent failure to meet a child's basic physical and/or psychological needs, and this is likely to result in the serious impairment of a child's mental health and/or development. It may involve a failing to provide adequate food, shelter or clothing, appropriate medical care or treatment. It may also include neglect of, or unresponsiveness to, a child's basic emotional needs.

A neglected child is a deprived child. Studies found that adopted Romanian children who had suffered concerted neglect were much less able to recognise familiar people and never felt any security or protection.[5] They had closed themselves down and were unable to feel the warmth or happiness of their adopted families. This was due to the neglect that they suffered as very small children. Obviously, children in our country don't suffer extreme neglect in this way but the study illustrates how neglect is linked to low self-worth and this will manifest itself as depression. In this busy world it is easy to neglect a child because they don't recognise neglect but take on the belief that they are not worth the attention.

Ignoring a child is a form of emotional neglect. This includes the parent or carer not responding to the child, not calling the child by his name, refusing to touch the child, withholding affection, failing to express warmth, failing to show interest in the child's feelings, thoughts or actions. According to the Prevent Child Abuse New York organisation, indicators of a neglected child include: sucking, biting, or rocking, destructive behaviour to self and/or others, depression, extremes in behaviour, aggressive or withdrawn behaviour, phobias, sleep disorders, mental or emotional developmental delays and anti-social behaviour such as cruelty, vandalism, stealing or cheating.

Physical neglect may be the consequence of lack of concern and/or poverty. Children who receive an inadequate diet, lack clean hygienic conditions and severe infestations are examples of physical neglect. But also, children allowed to live in dangerous conditions with no safety boundaries or

---

5 A. B. Wismer Fries and S. D. Pollak, 'Emotion understanding in post-institutionalised Eastern European children development and psychopathology', Emotion Research Group at the University of Wisconsin, 16 (2004), 355–69

who are left to harm themselves or at risk of being harmed by others must also be considered.

Not taking care of the child's physical wellbeing can be overlooked and even, at times, not recognised. For example, allowing them to stay up late results in tired and groggy children. This will leave them feeling low but also they will act up and be harder to manage the next day. One study has shown that there is a clear link between not getting enough sleep and the onset of depression.[6] Yet, according to the National Sleep Foundation's US 2004 *Sleep in America* poll, about 69 per cent of children aged ten and under experience some type of sleep problem. Starting with a good night's sleep could see a change in children's wellbeing.

Tip: Tell your child about all the people in his extended family who love him.

Emotional Abuse

Emotional abuse is the persistent emotional ill treatment of a child, which causes severe and persistent adverse effects on the child's emotional development. It may involve conveying to the child that he is worthless or unloved or inadequate.

Emotional abuse might be put across by letting the child feel that he will only be valued by meeting an adult's needs. When the child feels that he is only worthy if he meets high expectations that an adult has placed upon him, the pressure to succeed may be enough to tip him into depression. This is exploitation of the child and is not taking into account the child's personal ability, which may fall far short of the adult's expectation. Here are some other examples of emotional abuse:

---

6 Department of Public Health, School of Medicine, Nihon University, Tokyo, Japan, 'The relationship between depression and sleep disturbances: a Japanese nationwide general population survey', *J. Clinical Psychiatry*, 67:2 (2006), 196–203

- ignoring the child with a consistent failure to respond to the child's need for stimulation, nurturing, encouragement and protection
- failure to acknowledge the child's presence
- withholding affection
- belittling the child constantly
- rejecting by refusing to respond to the child's needs
- isolating the child from normal social contact
- verbally assaulting the child
- threatening the child with extreme punishment or threatening him with abandonment
- exploiting the child by encouraging him to take part in destructive, illegal or anti-social behaviour
- chronic parental arguing in the child's presence

Emotional abuse robs the child of a sense of security and can leave the child feeling frightened or that he is in constant danger. The sense of security that enables children to thrive and enjoy the outside world is obvious and easily recognisable. They laugh and squeal, become wrapped up in games, love to thrive at school, enjoy socialising with other children and can lose themselves in activities on their own. Once this is withdrawn, a child's delicate self-esteem can be grossly undermined and can lead to impaired development and depression.

One of the major problems with children who have suffered emotional abuse is aggression and cruelty. This is related to one primary problem in children: a lack of empathy. The ability for the child to emotionally 'understand' the impact of their behaviour on others is impaired in these children. They really do not understand or feel what it is like for others when they do or say something that hurts another. Indeed, these children often feel compelled to lash out and hurt others – most typically something less powerful than they are. They will hurt animals, smaller children, peers and siblings. One of the most disturbing elements of this aggression is that it is often accompanied by a detached, cold lack of empathy. They may show an intellectual response like regret but not an emotional response like remorse.

However, the worry is that if a parent suffered emotional abuse as a child then it could continue in their parenting style. The way our parents treated us is usually the only model we have for parenting. So we may not be aware of what a child needs because we base it on what we received as a child, but this information may be outdated. The good news is that there are plenty of resources available to give parents advice on how to meet their children's emotional needs – turn to the back of the book for a list of useful resources.

Tip: Go for a walk and collect leaves and twigs etc. for your child to make a picture with.

Physical Abuse

Physical abuse involves hitting, slapping, shaking or otherwise causing physical harm to a child. Extensive data from CHILDREN 1ST, the Royal Scottish Society for Prevention of Cruelty to Children, has shown that children who are frequently hit are more aggressive and more prone to developing emotional and mental health problems, particularly depression.

It's not simply the smack that can cause these problems; it is the violation that accompanies the smack that is so frightening. When a child is smacked the space around them has been invaded and they know they have no power to stop the assault. Children generally believe they have deserved it and will always be in fear of being hit again. This can cause a tightening of the child's defences, making it impossible for him to feel free and unbounded, which can lead to a chronic depression so subtle that it might not even be noticed. It's no different to us being in constant fear of being assaulted and knowing there is nothing we could do about it.

A parent who hits a child was usually hit himself as a child. The justification, 'Well, a smack never hurt anyone' is looking less and less sturdy. One study found that children who are spanked frequently were substantially more likely to have behaviour problems in school and suffered from both depression and anxiety.[7]

But if we blindly believe that smacking is acceptable because that's what our parents did then we are uninformed. Our parents smacked us because that was what everyone did but times have changed and smacking is becoming recognised as unacceptable, especially if it contributes to a child's depression.

Parents who use physical punishment may say they control the force of the smack and do not intend to harm their child. But the reality is that adults usually resort to smacking when they are angry and have 'lost it', which gives them less control over their actions. And the children are aware of it. Research by Save the Children looked at the opinions of 1,319 children and most of them believed that hitting was the result of a parent's feelings of anger, stress and frustration, rather than a reasonable act, and most described feeling distressed when they were hit.[8]

---

7 E.P. Slade, L.S. Wissow, Johns Hopkins Bloomberg School of Public Health, Department of Health Policy and Management, Baltimore, MD, 'Spanking in early childhood and later behavior problems: a prospective study of infants and young toddlers', *Pediatrics*, 133:5 (May 2004), 1321–30
8 E. Cutting, 'It doesn't sort anything: a report on the views of children and young people about the use of physical punishment', Edinburgh: Save the Children, (2001)

The American Academy of Paediatrics offers a strategy for effective discipline requiring three essential components:

1. a positive, supportive, loving relationship between the parent(s) and child,
2. use of positive reinforcement strategies to increase desired behaviours, and
3. removing reinforcement or applying punishment to reduce or eliminate undesired behaviours.

All components must be functioning well for discipline to be successful.

Tip: Tell your child that he's going to have so much fun today and you will put the 'have fun' thought into his head.

Sexual Abuse

Sexual abuse is an outright contravention of a child's innocence. Sexual abuse can be the unthinkable: forcing or enticing a child or young person to take part in sexual activities, whether or not the child is aware of what is happening, which may involve physical contact, including penetrative or non-penetrative acts. They may include non-contact activities, such as involving children in looking at, or in the production of, pornographic material or watching sexual activities or encouraging children to behave in sexually inappropriate ways.

A child's verbal allegations must always be treated with the greatest respect. Children are entitled to be listened to and to have their allegations treated seriously. Although there can be occasions when children invent allegations, as a result of adult pressures or for a variety of other reasons, research suggests that such fabricated allegations are rare and that children are, in fact, more likely to claim they are not being assaulted when they are than vice versa.

Symptoms of sexual abuse

These symptoms differ from child to child, depending on both their environment and specific situation.

For primary school children the effects may show by:
* ✳ Sexually explicit play and behaviour
* ✳ Becoming very clingy
* ✳ Wetting and soiling
* ✳ Delayed language and development
* ✳ Eating and sleeping problems
* ✳ As if out of control at times
* ✳ Poor concentration
* ✳ Becoming withdrawn or aggressive
* ✳ Avoiding adults

For secondary school children they also may show the following symptoms:
* ✳ Sexually precocious behaviour and prostitution
* ✳ Sexual abuse of other children
* ✳ Changes in school performance
* ✳ Isolation from peers

Sexual abuse can also take place verbally. Pointed remarks about the child's pubertal development whether it be teasing about an adolescent girl's budding breasts or a boy's lack of hair on his face can be overstepping the line. Games based around a child's sexual maturing can be transgressing their boundaries. For example, a dad flirting with his daughter or a mum paying too much attention to a son's body can feel extremely uncomfortable to an adolescent. Unless they are strong, and can set their own limits with their parents, they may withdraw from the relationships and this can prelude depression.

If you suspect that your child has been sexually abused, the first thing to do is remain calm. Even if you feel shocked, don't convey this to your child; this will protect him from further distress. The two most important things to do first are to give him a big hug and tell him he did the right thing in telling you and secondly to tell him that he is not to blame. There is a whole course of suggested action that is brilliantly outlined for parents who have just discovered their child has been abused. This is available from the National Society for the Prevention of Cruelty to Children and whose contact details are available at the end of this book.

The most important thing you can do to help your child from ever being sexually abused is to empower him. You do this by discussing sexual matters from a young age. Talking about bodies and how they function is a normal part of parenting and there are some great books to be found in the children's section of the library which can help you to get the right pitch for the appropriate age group. You also explain to him that he has a right to not allow anyone to touch his body if he doesn't wish them to. If he hears this enough he will recognise that when someone touches him, and he doesn't like it, he can say 'No' and walk away. This is probably the single most important message he will hear that will help to keep him safe from harm.

Tip: Tell your child how proud you are of the way he handled himself when he was in a difficult situation.

Parental Depression

Romance fails us and so do friendships, but the relationship of parent and child, less noisy than all the others, remains indelible and indestructible, the strongest relationship on earth.

Theodore Reik, writer

There is a strong link between depression in parents and their children, according to a study in the January 2001

American Journal of Psychiatry ('Patterns of psychopathology and dysfunction in high-risk children of parents with panic disorder and major depression'). When parents have major depression, their children are at risk of emotional and behavioural problems of their own. When depression in parents is diagnosed, the children are often not even considered but it makes complete sense that the child would be affected as well as the adult.

In my case, my son Gregory was depressed at about five years old but I didn't notice until one day he said, 'I feel like a brick in that wall.' I thought I had been doing a good job by taking care of his needs. I even employed someone to help a few hours a week so I could have some time off and I chose a nice woman who adored him and would love him up. But when he made that statement I was devastated. I knew I was missing out on something for him and even though I was very depressed at the time, my panic got me in such a state that I knew I had to seek some help.

Once I started talking with experts in child depression I began to grasp the principles outlined in this book and that I had to start focusing on him as much as myself. I think I had felt so bad in life that my head was drawn downwards and I was unable to see the negative effect this was having on Gregory. But now I can see that I just wasn't in his life; I wasn't in the centre of his world. I was paying lip service to parenting him and he felt my neglect. It was because I had so little to give myself and so little to give him that he felt my distance.

Our recovery was a joint affair. And in fact, parenting Gregory through his recovery made it so much easier to parent myself through my own recovery because in parenting him I felt I was also giving to myself. For example, I tried to make the most of the fresh air and, as we lived by the beach, I took lots of picnics down there and spent a lot of time playing in rock pools. Instead of muttering to myself,

'Oh I'm so bored,' I began to get into Gregory's world by feeling the childlike wonder that I had denied myself when I was a child. I learned to have so much fun with him and we grew very close in the following few years and we both fully recovered. This closeness has stayed with us since and we (most of the time!) are good friends.

Tip: Have a quiet five minutes with your child and talk over something that you both took part in.

Conflict within families

In each family a story is playing itself out, and each family's story embodies its hope and despair.

Auguste Napier

Living in a family which undergoes conflict can be very stressful for children and this has been confirmed by researchers at Columbia University in New York City, who reported that negative parenting may put children at a higher risk for anxiety and depression.[9] The investigators interviewed nearly six hundred parents and their children, and results showed that poor parental behaviours – such as verbal abuse, inconsistent rules, parental arguments in front of children and a lack of supervision – can all increase the chances of childhood anxiety or depression.

And the conflict is not just the big stuff, i.e. verbal abuse or constant rows. It can be just as stressful to live amongst niggling or sniping. I have sat in a kitchen and felt the tension when a couple are getting at each other and you could cut it with a knife. I felt for the children because I could get out but they couldn't. Another type of conflict

---

9 D. Cicchetti and D. J. Cohen (eds.), *Developmental Psychopathology: Risk, disorder, and adaptation*, Volume 3 (2nd edition), New York, Wiley, 2003

is when one parent contains hidden anger – covert but powerful. Children learn to behave in a way that won't upset the balance and tip the parent into a rage. This type of learned behaviour is very stifling and, over time, can cause a child to emotionally shut down.

Research from the University of Michigan (Department of Psychiatry, 2003) shows that family conflict can trigger depression in children and adolescents. Moreover it shows that family conflict also slows down the recovery process, which can complicate matters. But it has also been shown that if the whole family is able to receive some guidance and support, this is not only useful for the family but very helpful to the depressed child.

Tip: Give your child a sense of responsibility by giving him a daily job in the family.

Junk food

Junk food can seriously affect a child's mood. A pioneering nutrition and mental health programme, thought to be the only one of its kind in Britain, was carried out at Rotherham, South Yorkshire and the results were published in January 2006. According to Caroline Stokes, its research nutritionist, the mental health patients she saw (which includes those with depression) generally had the poorest diets she had ever come across. 'They are commonly eating lots of convenience foods, snacks, takeaways, chocolate bars, crisps. It's very common for clients to be drinking a litre or two of fizzy drinks a day. They get lots of sugar but a lot of them are eating only one portion of fruit or vegetable a day, if that.'

But it's not just what a child eats that can leave them depressed. The Mental Health Foundation published a report (January 2006) that stated not only have studies linked junk food to depression but also the absence of essential fats, vitamins and minerals in our diets. It's so easy to 'satisfy' a child with a chocolate bar, crisps or some fast food to keep them happy. It's what they ask for and it seems to be what they enjoy but the price of this could be their emotional health.

The food industry is not helping matters. Celebrity endorsements, film sponsorship, magazines, posters and the internet are encouraging children to eat badly, even though they know they should choose fruit and vegetables. Children also agree. They have said in one study that the government should restrict advertising of unhealthy food and drink and give better promotion to healthy alternatives.[10] But the modern marketers are extremely successful at giving processed foods the 'fun factor' and this can make it difficult for us to dissuade our children to eat less of it.

What is so great about children is that they learn so fast about food and its link to how they feel. If you start talking about it yourself when you notice you don't feel good after an over indulgent meal, they will pick up on the challenge and notice the same thing happening in themselves. If they feel grumpy you can ask them if the bag of sweets that they munched earlier has anything to do with how they feel now. You will be sowing seeds to help them to take better care of themselves.

Top Five Bad Mood Foods
The top five Bad Mood Foods are sugar, white flour, fats, dairy products and salt. This is mainly what junk food is made from but the fallout from eating it is still widely underestimated. Eating enough junk food can create havoc

---

10 National Children's Bureau, 'Children's views on non-broadcast food and drink advertising', Report for the Office of the Children's Commissioner, September 2006

in the body, enough havoc to create anxiety, fatigue, mood swings, irritability and severe depression. Here are some brief explanations why:

Sugar: It is estimated that every man, woman and child in the West eats the equivalent of a teaspoon of refined sugar every hour. Apart from the obvious sugars that we put in our food and drink, this is due to the vast amounts of sugar in processed food. For example, Sugar Puffs, which are marketed as 'nutritional', are 49 per cent sugar!

When we eat sugar and we feel that sugar 'rush', the body is trying to compensate for the large amount of unnatural glucose it has received by releasing sizeable amounts of insulin into the bloodstream. This has the effect of making a child feel 'high' for a short time and is often mistaken for a spurt of energy. Within an hour or so you may notice the downside in the child. They will seem listless, irritable and depressed and this is because the blood-sugar level has crashed.

White flour: White flour is so refined that it has been milled and robbed of its original, natural elements such as fibre, healthy oils, vitamins and minerals. In fact it is so depleted of nutrition that manufacturers are required by law to add calcium and B vitamins. Bread made from white flour has a very high GI factor, which means that it converts to sugar very quickly in the body, and too much sugar causes a sudden flood of unnatural glucose by releasing large amounts of insulin into the body. Rather like sugar, the effect will leave your child groggy, listless and depressed.

Fats: And it's saturated fats we are talking about – the ones in junk food. Excess levels of triglyceride found in blood fats are high and research undertaken at the Cholesterol

Centre of the Jewish Hospital in Cincinnati USA found that high cholesterol levels are not only bad for the heart but are dreadful for the brain. They are strongly correlated with the frequency of affective disorders like depression.

Dairy products: These are also high in cholesterol and so they will again negatively impact on a child's mood. But, indirectly, the dairy products that we feed our children also contain large amounts of sugar and so we have the double effect. Yoghurts are particularly high in sugar as well as mousses, creamed rice puddings, branded dairy desserts and the new range of 'smoothies' that look like they are all fruit but can contain lots of sugar as well as dairy products. It's worth reading the label before buying something you may think looks healthy. Keeping these types of puddings back for a weekend treat rather than an everyday food helps to stay within the 80/20 guide (eating well 80 per cent of the time balances out eating processed foods 20 per cent of the time).

Salt: Too much salt inhibits the kidney function and unhappy kidneys can lead to depression and fatigue. How much salt should a child have? According to the government, these are the guidelines:

> 4 to 6 years – 3g salt a day (1.2g sodium)
> 7 to 10 years – 5g salt a day (2g sodium)
> 11 and over – 6g salt a day (2.5g sodium)

Three grams of salt is about half a level teaspoon but did you know that 75 per cent of the salt we eat comes in processed foods such as breakfast cereals, soups, sauces, ready meals and biscuits? A well-known packet of salt and vinegar crisps contains one gram of salt. While this might not sound like a lot, it's almost half of the maximum recommended total daily intake for a six-year-old in just one snack.

And children love junk food – or do they? There is opinion that eating junk food is addictive and children are simply hooked on it and, in the absence of other foods, will crave it. A number of studies have been carried out in rats to look at junk foods and addiction. Dr Ann Kelley, professor of neuroscience at Wisconsin University, has been studying rats and diet for a number of years. One study found that a high-fat diet appears to alter the brain biochemistry in a similar way to drugs such as morphine.[11] They say this is due to the release of opioids – chemicals in the brain – that reduce the feeling of being full.

According to Dr Ann Kelley, rats 'love the high-fat food and they eat and eat. We found there are actually brain changes that are elicited by exposure to a chronic high-fat diet.' She believes that it is possible to compare the findings about rats to humans, making it very plausible that humans can become addicted to high-sugar and fatty foods.

But the evidence that good wholesome food can actually make you feel great and lift your depression is also available. I have covered all angles of this debate in *Superfoods To Boost Your Mood* and would highly recommend a read if you think that junk food maybe contributing to your child's depression.

And finally, there is the obesity issue. Britons are the fattest people in Europe and if current trends continue, the British Medical Association says, by 2020 some 30 per cent of boys and 40 per cent of girls in Britain will be clinically obese. Not only does obesity physically have a depressive effect, but the teasing from the child's peer group will have a detrimental effect on his self-esteem. There are some great recipes to try in Chapter 3 under 'Nourishing the Body'.

---

11 A. E. Kelley, B. A. Baldo and W.E. Pratt, 'A proposed hypothalamic-thalamic-striatal axis for the integration of energy balance, arousal and food reward', *J. Comp. Neurosci.* 493 (2005), 72–85

Being bullied

I wasn't being bullied at school at this point. I had a group of friends, and I was isolated because I wasn't communicating with my parents. I wasn't telling them what I was going through.
Randy Harrison, American actor

Depression can be a psychological symptom of a child who has been bullied. A study published in the *British Medical Journal* stated that adolescents who are being bullied and those who are bullies are at an increased risk of depression and suicide.[12] Interestingly, it confidently stated that it was the bullies who were as much at risk as those who were bullied. Another piece of research posted in the *British Medical Journal* stated that although bullies tended to be unhappy with school, children who were bullied tended to like school but tended to feel alone.[13] Bullying leaves children feeling vulnerable and frightened and if they also feel alone with their problem, they are at a high risk of depression.

The instance of bullying is rife and on the increase. The Children's Commissioner, Al Aynsley-Green, told the BBC in November 2006 that bullying is a scourge of childhood. He stated that new research just published reveals 20,000 children skip school every day because of bullies. In Ireland, one study showed that 34.5 per cent of children interviewed had a history of being bullied during their schooling.[14]

---

12 'Bullying, depression, and suicidal ideation in Finnish adolescents: school survey', *BMJ*, 319: 7206 (7 August 1999), 348–51

13 'Bullying behaviour and psychosocial health among school students in New South Wales, Australia: cross-sectional survey', *BMJ*, 319: 7206 (7 August 1999), 344–8

14 *Irish Journal of Psychological Medicine*, Department of Child and Family Psychiatry at the Mater Hospital in Dublin and UCD, (December 2004)

But it isn't always easy to find out if your child is being bullied. Some younger children may not even recognise that they are being bullied or they are not able to articulate their feelings and the first you may know of the problem is when your child suddenly doesn't want to go to school, or says they are ill when PE lessons are on the agenda.

Other symptoms can be:

- Coming home with cuts and bruises
- Torn clothes
- Asking for stolen possessions to be replaced
- 'Losing' dinner money
- Falling out with previously good friends
- Being moody and bad tempered
- Being quiet and withdrawn
- Wanting to avoid leaving the house
- Aggression with brothers and sisters
- ✳ Doing less well at schoolwork
- Insomnia

The worst thing to do is to overreact and storm into school demanding action. However, there are some fantastic resources at the back of this book to help you with your child if you think he is being bullied. Helping your child to deal with a bully can be a powerful learning tool because they will come across bullies for the rest of their lives and learning to deal with them at a young age can empower them towards a confident and safe outcome.

Tip: When your child laughs, tell him how it lights up your day.

Overindulgence

Human beings are the only creatures that allow their children to come back home.

Bill Cosby, actor

We've all experienced the overindulged child. That's the child that screams at his parent to '...get it...' and to '... get it now...' and then the parent does whatever it takes to calm him down. It's almost frightening to watch a child have so much power over a parent and the whole affair is so demeaning to both of them. Overindulgence is not quite the same as spoiling. When we refer to a child as spoiled, we usually describe behaviours that annoy the adults. While an overindulged child may act spoiled, the results of overindulgence are more far reaching. It hinders children from doing their developmental tasks and from learning necessary life lessons. Overindulging is the process of giving things to children to meet the adult's needs, not the child's. When the adult gives in to the unacceptable demands of the child, it is for the adult's peace of mind, not for the welfare of the child.

Overindulged children grow up in an unrealistic world and, as a result, they fail to learn skills such as perseverance, coping with failure in effective ways and getting along with others. Parents only ever overindulge a child to meet their own needs, not the needs of their children. For example, they may have grown up in a very poor family and, as a result, shower their children with excessive material wealth because they do not want their children to have the same poverty-stricken experience. Giving too much can be as destructive as giving too little. Overfilling with food, overbuying gifts that are unnecessary are ways of indulging a child to the point of 'stuffing' them. If you look at an overstuffed child you can see they aren't content; they are full up, not in a gentle way but in a needy, greedy way. I know myself if I eat a lot and then feel bloated, the bloated feeling wears off but my appetite has increased and I need more food to get the same sort of satisfaction. This same scenario is what happens to children when they are overindulged. It's as if the clear line of what is acceptable is being continually shifted and the child's craving moves with the line. But it all takes place for the benefit of the adult, not the child, and if it continues, the child will become depressed because its appetite will never be satisfied.

Once I was in a small shop and a woman came in and started browsing. The woman's daughter was waiting outside the shop with a dog when she peered through the door and shouted, 'Mum, let me look at that jumper.' The mother murmured something like 'OK, in a minute.' The daughter screamed, 'GET IT NOW!' The mother didn't hesitate; she picked up the jumper and took it to the doorway for the girl to look at. 'Nah,' said the girl, dismissing the item, and the mother returned it to the rail after which they both left. The shock in the shop was palpable and there were mutterings of 'the youth today', 'she's unbelievable', 'if she were my daughter she would get a good slap on the legs'. This situation is the product of an overindulged child and that child will struggle to be accepted in the adult world, demanding that others adhere to her commands and expecting them to compromise themselves in order to make her happy. She will probably feel victimised if her requirements aren't met by others and they won't be because when this girl has to fend for herself in the real world she will find that people won't bow to her orders like her mother did. She will have to go through much soul-searching to find an inner peace and lasting happiness.

ADHD

Between my dyslexia and ADHD, it was a miracle that I made it through school at all.

Brian Walker, American inventor

ADHD – Attention Deficit Hyperactivity Disorder. What is it? Well, no one really knows. There are no blood tests to validate this condition and even the experts are arguing about exactly what ADHD is. Dr Fred A. Baughman Jr, a board-certified neurologist and child neurologist and Fellow of the American Academy of Neurology, said, 'In calling ADHD an abnormality/disease, without scientific facts, the psychiatrist knowingly lies, and violates the informed consent rights of both patient and parents. This is de facto medical malpractice.' Controversial? Yes. But, what we do know is the numbers of children being diagnosed with ADHD are now up to 1 in 20! That is one big problem. And what is the NHS treatment for ADHD? It's a drug called Ritalin, which has the same effect as something in between amphetamine and cocaine! There has got to be another way to treat our children.

There are some symptoms of ADHD that run along the same lines as a child who is disruptive, depressed and obviously unhappy. Studies indicate approximately 30 per cent of those with ADHD also suffer from depression. One such study is *The Multimodal Treatment Study of Children with Attention Deficit Hyperactivity Disorder.* The first findings from this study, which were published by the National Institute of Mental Health in December 1999, suggest that up to a third of children with ADHD also have depression, and that children who have ADHD are three times as likely to have depression as children who don't. Because depression is hard to diagnose in children, rates in children with ADHD vary widely.

According to the NHS, there are three signs of ADHD – not paying attention, being overactive and acting without thinking. A child can have symptoms of all three. However, to be diagnosed with ADHD a child must have:

- Six or more symptoms of **not paying attention** (inattention) **And**
- Six or more symptoms of **being overactive** (hyperactivity) and **acting before thinking** (impulsivity).

Talking too much and fidgeting, for example, can both be symptoms of hyperactivity. What is 'Not paying attention'?

For inattentive children:

- Often pay no attention to detail and make careless mistakes in schoolwork or other activities
- Can't concentrate on one game or task for long
- Often seem not to listen when spoken to
- Often don't follow instructions, and fail to finish schoolwork and tasks around the house
- Often have difficulty organising tasks and activities
- Often avoid tasks that need a lot of concentration
- Often lose things
- Are easily distracted
- Are often forgetful

What is being 'overactive'?

Either hyperactive:

- Often fidget or squirm when sitting down
- Keep getting up
- Often run about or climb instead of sitting still
- Often have difficulty playing quietly
- Are on the go all the time, and act as if driven by a motor
- Talk too much

Or impulsive:

✳ Often blurt out answers before a question is finished
✳ Often have difficulty waiting their turn
✳ Often interrupt others

But, just because your child has lots, or even all, of the symptoms listed above it doesn't mean he or she has ADHD. Doctors also look for the following:

✳ Your child must have been behaving like this for at least six months
✳ Some of the symptoms must have been present before your child reached the age of seven years old
✳ Above all, your child's behaviour must be causing problems in at least two places (for example, at home and at school)

Before diagnosing ADHD your doctor will also check that your child's symptoms are not caused by another condition such as depression, an anxiety disorder or a personality disorder.

If we look at the child who is diagnosed with ADHD and treat him as if he were depressed, we might go a long way to help him in all these areas. Stephen Faraone, PhD of Harvard Medical School, Boston, Massachusetts, reviewed the patterns of depression in ADHD.[15] Because you can have ADHD with other conditions, there has been controversy as to whether it exists as a primary condition or only secondary to other syndromes such as depression. Depressed patients demonstrate diminished concentration and individuals with depression often manifest themselves in physical agitation

15 S. V. Faraone, 'Patterns of co-morbidity in ADHD: artifact or reality?' Program and abstracts of the 154th Annual Meeting of the American Psychiatric Association, 5–10 May 2001, New Orleans, Louisiana. Industry Symposium 46B

and distractibility. It may be difficult to differentiate these symptoms from the symptoms of ADHD.

One study published in the *American Journal of Public Health* has shown that 30 per cent of children with ADHD also have depression.[16] Children with ADHD are unable to stay focused on a task, cannot sit still, act without thinking and rarely finish anything, which is what depressed children may also do. A study published in the *Journal of Affective Disorders*[17] examined the course of depression in 76 children with ADHD in order to learn more about the relationship between ADHD and depression. The authors were especially interested in whether depression in children with ADHD represents an actual clinical depression, or whether it may be better understood as a kind of 'demoralisation', which can result from the day-to-day struggles that children with ADHD often have.

Whichever way round it happens, depression is a powerful factor in children with ADHD and the treatment that this book sets out to help a child with depression can only be beneficial for a child with ADHD.

Tip: Find something funny and just laugh: your child will laugh with you.

Parental pressure

We can't form our children on our own concepts; we must take them and love them as God gives them to us.
                                    Johann Wolfgang Von Goethe, writer

Today's society is highly achievement orientated, and – rightly or wrongly – many parents feel that unless they

---

16 Kuo and Faber Taylor, 94:9, 1580
17 'Attention deficit hyperactivity disorder and affective disorders in childhood: continuum, co-morbidity or confusion', (January 1998), 113–122

subject their children to constant pressure, they'll end up as losers. We want our children to do well, excel at school, in sports and socially. At the same time, children are getting a message about achievement, failure and pressure from many other sources: other children, other parents, school and the media – in other words, from just about every corner of their world. The message is 'If you fail, it will be awful for you and for us as well. Don't let us all down.' They don't need to get this from parents to be affected by it, but if the parents buy into it, it can multiply the pressure a child feels many times over.

A sensitive child who becomes anxious and afraid of failure will be at risk of depression and become discouraged. They develop a view of themselves as an 'I can't' child. This type of child tends to give up without trying. There may be tearfulness, whining and a stubborn refusal to take any kind of risk or try anything new.

Other children become under-achievers. They usually take up another trait to mask their fear of failure. They may state 'I don't care' or become the class joker. They may try to be as inconspicuous as possible and have a way of quietly treading water, making sure they don't fail but also never really trying for success.

The reasons for under-achieving are many, but one of them is, paradoxically, the fear of failure or of encouraging expectations that seem too high to achieve. When I was young my mother piled on the academic pressure to a point where I just couldn't work. My head was in a fog and I couldn't think clearly. Worse still, when I passed my 11-plus with 'flying colours' it was clear that I wasn't stupid but very 'lazy'. But I wasn't. I loved achieving in other areas but the academic pressure was too high.

Some children become rebels, particularly in adolescence but often children become deeply depressed. If their whole sense of worth is ripped away because they didn't do well enough, it will be hard for them to feel happy. And, it's not just academic pressure but the pressure to perform at home. It is often a pressure to be 'good' but being good is hard for a child. If the pressure is there to behave in a rigid environment they will become anxious about saying and doing the wrong thing and this will become normal.

The pressure from parents is always to meet the needs of the parents, not the child and the pressuring of children may begin even before they go to school, because the majority of parents are placing their children into mainstream education, which is a system of high-achievement pressure.

Competitive activities like tests and exams may help to motivate children and develop self-discipline, but there are other ways to do this too. The extent to which competitive sport encourages teamwork can also be overrated – it doesn't, necessarily. Individualism is what it encourages. Certainly, these things have a place, but perhaps not the place of pre-eminence that they have so often been given. It is in the interests of child wellbeing that parents and those who are for children, speak out about practices that pressurise and stress kids unnecessarily.

We all want our children to do well and we know that if they don't keep up with their peers then they will fall behind and this may make them appear unable to cope with the system and so there is more pressure to catch up. The pressure at school is enough for any child and when they come back home they need to be supported by the family.

Deepak Chopra, the author of many books on spiritual living, once said in an interview that he did not want to academically pressure his children. Instead he fostered an awareness of enjoying studying and rather than trying to meet the school's targets, got his children to set their own goals which they could work towards. It was a great risk because he did not pester his children at all about how they were getting on; he just let them take responsibility for their own academic path with his full support and encouragement. He also told his children that he would support them financially when they became adults to take any pressure off them. When I heard that, I decided to take a similar approach with my children. What a huge gamble – what if they fail? So far, so good. My seventeen-year-old son is a grade-A student and plans to go to medical school. We will see how it turns out but one thing I do know, he is much happier at school than I was.

Tip: Don't look at your watch when your child has your attention.

Peer pressure

Being popular and fitting in is what counts for every teenager across the globe. Peer pressure is intense and has an impact on many undesirable choices that many teenagers are making – whether or not to smoke, drink, have sex, attend school, indulge in criminal/antisocial behaviour, for example. Conforming to their peers can become an everyday task and since teenagers can exaggerate the smallest of decisions or tasks into life-altering events, the pressure can feel intolerable.

Peer pressure also can turn the best child into a coward and can lead them to do things that we know the child would never choose to do on their own. While not all peer pressure is bad, the type of peer pressure that leaves a child feeling confused or hurt is never good. When peer pressure is good it is very, very good, but when it is bad it can be devastating.

Peer pressure starts from the moment the child gets to school and continues through to ... well, I know I'm *still* influenced by a crowd! If the child has a shaky self -esteem, he could be much more likely to bend towards what his contemporaries are up to in order to gain their approval and to bolster his own of sense of worth.

The 'Chemical Imbalance' Debate

There is a wide and controversial debate about what causes depression and what is an effective treatment. The medical profession, in general, believes that depression is the result of a chemical imbalance in the brain; specifically they refer to a lack of serotonin in the brain. Serotonin is a chemical messenger that affects emotions, behaviour and thought and facilitates communication between nerve cells. The medical profession believes that a lack of serotonin is directly responsible for depression and, by and large, this is what most drug treatments are based on.

However, it is also important to look at what is *not* said in the scientific literature. One study says that the evidence does not back up this claim. Its authors state: 'To our knowledge, there is not a single peer-reviewed article that can be accurately cited to directly support claims of serotonin deficiency in any mental disorder, while there are many articles that present counterevidence.'[18]

There is a growing voice that offers a different hypothesis and says, yes there is a chemical imbalance in the brain but it is as a result of the depression and not the other way round. Your brain processes emotions, thoughts, impressions and physical sensations by releasing chemicals. To say that depression is caused by a chemical imbalance is a contradiction in terms; your whole body relies on its own

18 Jeffrey R. Lacasse and Jonathan Leo, 'Serotonin and depression: a disconnect between the advertisements and the scientific literature', *Public Library of Science, US, Journal*, (8 November 2005)

internal chemistry to regulate everything: we are chemical! When you are happy, your brain releases endorphins, which are the chemicals that make you feel good. When you are depressed your brain sends signals to you in the form of chemicals to tell you that you are unhappy.

Thirty years ago depression in children was disbelieved; now it's the area for the fastest rate of increase in depression. Indeed, there is still very little known about the role of biology in depression but human biology doesn't advance this much in thirty years so there may be other reasons for the acceleration of the depression figures in children and teenagers.

The Pill Paradox

As far as antidepressants go, some have argued that as depression may be due to a deficiency of serotonin, by enhancing serotonin through the use of antidepressants, this improves the symptoms of depression. However, it could be argued that that's akin to saying that because a rash on one's leg gets better with the use of a steroid cream, the rash must be due to a steroid deficiency.

Regarding depression as 'just' a chemical imbalance wildly misconstrues the disorder.

Psychology Today, March 1999

In a controversial move, the European Medicines Agency announced in June 2006 that depressed children as young as eight could be given Prozac. But the guidelines from the National Institute for Health and Clinical Excellence (NICE), the body that provides national guidance on health treatments, indicate that for children with moderate to severe depression, individual or family therapy should be offered for at least three months. However, NICE also said that antidepressant medication should not be offered to children and young people with moderate to severe depression *except* in combination with therapy but it *can* be used when therapy is refused or there are *no therapy places available*. With the waiting times for therapy being up to one and half years, the options are limited!

There is a place for anti-depressants for anyone at risk of harming themselves; however, they are not the long-term answer for depression. If you have a bad tooth you take painkillers to temporarily suppress the pain but at some point you have to get to the dentist to have a look at the source of the pain and get it resolved otherwise you will be taking painkillers for a long time.

Three things to consider when considering antidepressants for children are:

1. The side effects of general antidepressants, which can include dry mouth, urinary retention, blurred vision, constipation, sedation, sleep disruption, weight gain, headaches, nausea and agitation

2. Coming off antidepressants can lead some children to have thoughts about suicide, which seem to be attributed to the antidepressants rather than the depression

3. If you are not confronting the source of the depression, the underlying causes, then when the child eventually comes of the antidepressants, the source of the depression will still be there

According to research, antidepressants are also much worse at preventing a relapse than the appropriate psychotherapy.[19] This substantiates the premise that the underlying causes must be tackled, alongside the symptoms, in order to help a

19 J. D. Teasdale, *et al.*, 'Prevention of relapse/recurrence in major clinical depression by mindfulness-based cognitive therapy', *Journal of Consulting and Clinical Psychology*, 68: 4 (2000), 615–23

child recover fully from his depressive state. One study has even stated that cognitive therapy (looking at the way we think) can be as effective as antidepressants even in severe depression.[20]

The problem is that the waiting list for all types of therapy are so long in some areas and if your child is depressed, you want immediate help. It's a minefield of controversy and whether you decide to go down the antidepressant route or not, the fundamental causes of the depression also need to be tackled and this is what this whole book is about – helping your child recover.

Tip: Ask 'What's troubling you?' rather than 'What's wrong with you?'

⋔ EFFECTS

Having looked at the causes of depression, we now look at the knock-on effects of depression. Generally speaking, when children are depressed they go into a survival mode. They don't sit down and discuss their feelings but they will act them out instead. They don't plan how to act out their feelings; instead they will take up modes of behaviour that are familiar to them. These behaviours will have been identified from their environment, be it through the family, school or their social

---

20 R. J. DeRubeis, S. D. Hollon, J. D. Amsterdam, R. C. Shelton, P. R. Young, R. M. Salomon, J. P. O'Reardon, M. L. Lovett, M. M. Gladis, L. L. Brown and R. Gallop, 'Cognitive therapy vs medications in the treatment of moderate to severe depression', Department of Psychology, University of Pennsylvania, Philadelphia, PA 19104, USA. July 2005: 'Cognitive therapy can be as effective as medications for the initial treatment of moderate to severe major depression, but this degree of effectiveness may depend on a high level of therapist experience or expertise.'

circle. They will take up behaviours that they have witnessed, read about or latched onto via peer pressure.

By undertaking the steps in 'Nurturing the Soul', you will be getting to the centre of the causes and helping to neutralise the depression. But it's a two-pronged attack because if your child is acting out their depression you also need identify *how* they are doing it and help them to recourse their actions.

There are many ways a child may act out their feelings that are worrying but not vital. These may include:

* Under-achieving at school
* Sleeping a lot
* Having no friends
* Not eating much
* Not exercising much
* Having no hobbies
* Acting moody etc.

However, there can be more extreme modes of acting out feelings that need to be attended to much more urgently. These extreme behaviours are usually carried out by older children – over eleven years old. However, this does not mean that younger children do not need as much time and effort spent on their recovery, it simply means that potentially harmful behaviour may need to be dealt with more urgently. This is why this book focuses on helping depressed children who act out in ways outlined in the following pages.

Self-harm
Self-harm is when someone deliberately hurts or injures him or herself.

This can take a number of forms including:

* Cutting
* Punching oneself

❀ Throwing their bodies against something
❀ Pulling out hair or eyelashes
❀ Scratching, picking or tearing at one's skin, causing sores
   and scarring
❀ Burning

Some young people self-harm on a regular basis while
others do it just once or a few times. For some people it is
part of coping with a specific problem and they stop once
the problem is resolved. Other people self-harm for years,
whenever certain kinds of pressures or feelings arise.

Self-harm is not the same as a suicide attempt. However,
self-harm is related to a diminishing sense of self-worth, in
the same way that suicide is, with suicide being the ultimate
expression. Self-harm may represent the prevention of a
suicide period by existing as an aversion strategy or a survival
strategy. It's hard to grasp but, as I understand it from
speaking to people who self-harm, it is undertaken to relieve
emotional pain. If the emotional pain is overwhelming
then self-harming is a way of focusing on physical pain and
numbing the emotional pain.

Young people who self-harm have often had very
difficult or painful experiences or relationships. These may
include:
❀ Bullying or discrimination
❀ Losing someone close to them such as a parent, brother,
   sister or friend
❀ Lack of love and affection or neglect by parents or carers
❀ Physical or sexual abuse
❀ A serious illness that affects the way they feel about
   themselves

Other young people may start to self-harm as a way of
dealing with the problems and pressures of everyday life.

Pressure can come from family, school and peer groups to conform or to perform well (for example, to get good exam results). Young people can feel angry, frustrated or bad about themselves if they cannot live up to other people's expectations. The expectations that mostly push young people to the limits are those from families that insist their children are not good enough. While talking to young people who self-harm, it often seemed that their self-harming started when they fell out with their parents. For example, Lipstick said, 'I first started to cut myself when me and my mum would get into fights – she would yell at me and the things she would tell me would hurt so much that I figured to take away this emotional pain I'll just make this pain into a physical one.'

Young people who self-harm usually have low self-esteem. For some this is linked to poor body image, eating disorders or drug misuse. Understanding why young people self-harm involves knowing as much as possible about their lives and lifestyles. Peer pressures may occasionally be the most important reason for self-harm. Young people may find themselves among friends or other groups who self-harm and may be encouraged or pressurised to do the same.

How common is self-harm?

It's impossible to say exactly how many young people self-harm because:

❉ Many young people hurt themselves secretly before finding the courage to tell someone

❉ Many of them never ask for counselling or medical help

❉ There is no standard definition of self-harm used in research

❉ There are no national statistics on self-harm currently available

However, evidence suggests that self-harm is most common in children over the age of eleven and increases in frequency with age. It is uncommon in very young children, although there is evidence of children as young as five trying to harm themselves. Self-harm is more common among girls and young women than boys and young men. Studies indicate that, among young people over thirteen years of age, approximately three times as many females as males harm themselves. According to the National Children's Bureau, a study in Oxford found that approximately 300 per 100,000 males aged between 15 and 24 years, and 700 per 100,000 females of the same age, were admitted to hospital following an episode of self-harm during the year 2000.

Warning signs

Warning signs that someone is injuring themselves include: unexplained frequent injury including cuts and burns, wearing long pants and sleeves in warm weather, low self-esteem, difficulty handling feelings, relationship problems and poor functioning at work, school or home.

How to help a child who is self-harming

Self-harm is almost always a symptom of another underlying problem. While a child is self-harming they are coping with that problem. One very, very important point to make is that people who self-harm sometimes have no control over it. I have talked to some young people who have harmed themselves and cannot remember doing it. Others have harmed themselves during a row with another and didn't notice until after the shouting had stopped. Asking them to stop self-harming without getting to the root cause of their problems is not helpful. Ultimately, we have little power over children harming themselves. They have to stop when they are ready and their recovery is very personal to them.

There are some excellent resources that offer many pointers for recovery and these are listed in the back of the book. Some internet forums are extremely helpful in getting children to talk to others about their experiences. The very shame of self-harming makes it extremely difficult for the child to discuss their issues with a professional; doctors will generally offer antidepressants (which maybe necessary in extreme cases) but the root of the problem still needs to be tackled.

What the child really wants is an adult who cares about them unconditionally, will not judge them for their actions and will accept the level of their pain as being so great that they are driven to self-abuse. The adult must completely accept this without judgement. Once the trust is established with the adult, the adult must help the child by putting in place some alternative coping mechanisms to be used with the self-harming and to eventually replace the self-harming. To demand the child stops self-harming immediately is not helpful and will only serve to sever the trust between the child and the adult.

Bearing in mind that the parent is not always the best person to be this adult with unconditional regard, it may be preferable for the adult to be someone who is shrewd and very knowledgeable about these issues. I recommend getting hold of a counsellor who is wise to self-harming. I know this is a difficult task because so many counsellors are so inexperienced and lacking the necessary skills, but there are some excellent people who you will find if you search hard enough. However, some people who have self-harmed have had bad experiences from professionals, including accident and emergency and psychiatric services, so you should not immediately assume that these services will be what they want. Ask them what they want to do and what help they would like to receive.

Some parents feel they have no choice but to get their child to a doctor as soon as possible. Ensure the doctor is familiar with self-harming and will not judge the child. You may only get one chance of talking about this issue with a child and if the acceptance isn't there the child may never talk about it again. They will be so on edge about whether or not they should discuss it in the first place that even so much as a raised eyebrow might put them off talking about it again.

As far as residential units go, there are very few units in the health service where the staff has the necessary training and experience to allow them to confront and manage this condition. Hence, the crisis recovery unit at London's Bethlem Royal Hospital is almost unique in the UK, offering a specialist service for those who suffer from self-injury. You may be able to gain access to it through your doctor.

Drinking/Drug Abuse

Drinking

All adolescents drink – or all the ones I meet do. It's a rite of passage to get drunk for the first time and every child does it. Going out with a friend and having a drink is commonplace and even if we don't like it, we have to accept it. However, there are certain boundaries that can be put in place to contain the drinking. These will differ according to each family but for my family, the sixteen-year-old is allowed two beers on a Friday night and two beers on a Saturday night and two if he goes out to a party. For a special lunch he will always be offered a glass of wine. This has gradually increased as he's grown older. The seven-year-old gets a splash of wine topped up with fruit juice. The amount varies according to each family's lifestyle and there is no hard and fast rule.

However, if a child is depressed then drinking can take on a whole new meaning.

Drinking among children is a common effect of depression. The initial age that children start drinking increases the risks of excess drinking in teenagers. A 2002 survey[21] of more than 14,000 students in secondary schools in England, Scotland and Wales, found that:

* 6 out of 10 boys and 50 per cent of girls aged 11–12 had tried at least one alcoholic drink
* Of this age group 9 per cent of boys and 5 per cent of girls described themselves as regular drinkers. This figure rises to 39 per cent of boys and 33 per cent of girls among 15–16-year-olds
* 8 out of 10 students aged 15–16 had drunk alcohol in the previous month
* 43 per cent of students aged 14–15 and 50 per cent of 15–16 year olds had consumed 5 or more alcoholic drinks in a single session
* More than 25 per cent of students aged 15–16 reported 3 or more binge-drinking sessions in the past month
* Over 60 per cent of students reported that they had drunk alcohol before the age of 13 and 1 in 7 students said that they began drinking at least once a week

These statistics have increased even between my writing the first and second draft of this book. The BBC's *Panorama* has stated 'The number of children admitted to hospital because of alcohol abuse has jumped over 20 per cent in the last five years, with ambulance crews regularly picking up kids who have drunk themselves senseless.'

---

21 B. Bates *et al.*, *Smoking, drinking and drug use among young teenagers in 2002: a survey carried out on behalf of the Department of Health by the National Centre for Social Research and the National Foundations for Educational Research*, (London, The Stationery Office, 2005)

Why do children turn to drink?

Children's attitudes and behaviour are initially shaped by families – both directly, in that parents act as role models and indirectly, in that levels of family support, control and conflict are linked to teenage drinking. A sensible drinking example set by parents seems to be particularly important, as both abstainers and heavy drinkers are more likely to have heavy-drinking children. Living with a parent or parents with an alcohol problem can have a significant impact on a young person. Alcohol misuse can be the root cause of familial dysfunction and this breakdown of family function can extend outside the family unit and affect relationships with the wider community.

Significantly, the children of problem drinkers have more problems than children of non-problem drinkers. Underachieving at school, emotional and psychological problems and anti-social behaviour are some of the difficulties that such young people can develop.

But sometimes the pain of depression is so bad that the child has to cope and alcohol numbs emotions. One thirteen-year-old boy told me 'When I drink I get a buzz and I stop feeling bad'; it's that simple – alcohol takes away the depression, albeit temporarily. The problem arises when the alcohol wears off and the depression comes back and he feels even worse because there is also a hangover to contend with which can also make you feel depressed. Once the cycle sets in a whole new set of problems arise such as violence when drinking, hanging around with other heavy drinkers and their influence on your child and becoming obsessive about getting another drink while losing sight of the rest of his life.

Peer pressure is also a big factor in persuading children to drink. This can be particularly pertinent if a child is unhappy because they may want to fit in with a peer group. They can allow themselves to be influenced to do things they would not consider doing on their own. Binge drinking is becoming more common and takes place in groups where it can be very hard for a child to resist the pack mentality. In fact, resisting any negative peer pressure is possibly the most difficult situation a child has to face.

Teaching him ways to handle that, from the very beginning, will give him the tools to make the right decisions. We can't choose our child's friends but we can help to guide him in the right direction by being open and direct about his choice of friends. If we tell our child that we like the friend but not their behaviour it will help the child to see there is a difference between the two and help him to judge the situation for his own benefit.

What to do if your child is drinking heavily

So, what do you do if your child is drinking more than he should? The bottom line is to build a stronger relationship between you and your child because this is the best way to influence him. Teenagers are much more likely to delay drinking when they feel they have a close, supportive tie with a parent. Furthermore, if your son or daughter eventually does begin to drink, a good relationship with you will help protect him or her from developing alcohol-related problems. If they have a strong bond with a parent, teenagers are apt to feel good about themselves and therefore are less likely to cave in to peer pressure to use alcohol.

The best way to address concerns about alcohol is to establish open communication about alcohol, the problems, the knock-on effects and how to drink safely. This may sound easier than it is in practice and your child may try to dodge any questions. Make sure you know exactly what you wish to discuss before you begin and don't give them your whole life experience in one sitting. Spread the conversations out and make it a natural conversation so that your child is more able to digest each piece of information you give him. Consider what you think his response may be before you start so you're prepared and don't drop your jaw when he reveals something shocking. If you make the conversation happen when you are both relaxed then it won't seem so intense and he may open up to you more than you expect.

Teenagers don't want to be out of control; they want to be contained and if they can't do it for themselves then it is up to us to teach them how to set good limits by doing it for them until they are able to do it for themselves. And, even though teenagers may not show it, they want to know that you care for them and that they are very important to you.

Drug abuse

It has long been recognised that there is a relationship between depression and illicit drug use. Exactly how they are related has been the subject of much debate and the main thrust of the argument is: what comes first, the depression or the drug abuse?

There is no conclusive evidence to finalise this question but it is thought that while drinking among adolescents is highly influenced by the family environment, drug taking is influenced mainly by life experiences outside the family setting. This means that parents often haven't got current knowledge about drug abuse, what drugs are fashionable, what the different type of drugs do and so on. For any family with a child who is taking drugs, the fear can be insurmountable and it is very easy for parents to become anxious and paranoid. But normal parental concern can become suspicion, which can lead to accusations or mistrust.

Here are some obvious warning signs:

✳ Money going missing or being spent with no clear evidence of what has been bought

❊ Suspicious substances or equipment lying around
❊ Lying or secretive behaviour
❊ Aggression

Knowing your child well, you may spot other more subtle
signs that their drug use is getting out of control:
❊ Sudden or regular mood changes
❊ Drowsiness
❊ Loss of appetite or interest in school, work or friends

Of course these changes in your child's personality may not
be connected to drugs. After all she or he is growing up
and adolescence is as powerful a force as many drugs! Ask
yourself: What makes me think drugs are involved? Only you
have the inside knowledge to answer that question.

The most common drug is cannabis. A study following
1,600 Australian schoolchildren aged fourteen to fifteen
for seven years found that while children who use cannabis
regularly have a significantly higher risk of depression, the
opposite was not the case – children who already suffered
from depression were not more likely than anyone else to
use cannabis. However, adolescents who used cannabis daily
were five times more likely to develop depression and anxiety
in later life.[22]

Many parents today are ambivalent about drugs such
as cannabis; some consider it to be relatively risk-free and
are more concerned about drugs such as cocaine or ecstasy.
However, cannabis is not a harmless drug. Depression,
anxiety and personality disturbances are all associated with
cannabis use. Research clearly demonstrates that cannabis use
has potential to cause problems in daily life, make a person's

22 'Mental health of teenagers who use cannabis', *British Journal of Psychiatry*,
180 (2002), 216–21

existing problems worse and increase the risk of psychosis.[23] Regular use also increases the possibility of the person using more 'hard' drugs like ecstasy, cocaine etc.

The majority of alcohol and drug abuse because of depression is taken up by adolescents. Although children under eleven do turn to substance use it is very rare. Whatever age the child, there is experimenting and then there are extremes of substance abuse. It is usually a phase but if it is anything more serious then intervention by a doctor may be necessary. There are residential places for adolescents who are addicted to substances available through NHS trusts and your child's GP will be the first port of call. In fact, there is currently a plethora of empty beds for residential treatment centres because doctors like to prescribe alternative drugs to help people to withdraw because it is less expensive. However, do enquire, with persistence, and contact the treatment centres directly. You can always feed back the details to your GP who can then follow them up on your behalf. Searching the internet is the fastest way to get this information.

What to do if your child starts taking drugs

For substance use that is critical, it is important to realise that no matter how much we want our child to stop using, we cannot *make* them. If a teenager wants to continue to use drugs and alcohol against parental wishes, he will find ways of getting it and hiding it. We can put in place some strong boundaries that draw the line of what behaviour is acceptable within the family and expect the child to adhere to the rules. If the child doesn't and has no money to buy substances, he

---

23 David M. Fergusson, L. John Horwood and Elizabeth M. Ridder, 'Tests of causal linkages between cannabis use and psychotic symptoms', *Journal of Addiction*, (March 2005)

may go onto crime to support his 'using'. You may need to move into a 'tough love' strategy which could involve facing the child with a series of aims that he has to achieve, such as giving up drugs and alcohol, or face being placed into a rehabilitation centre, getting a job or going back to school.

Single mother Angela had such a problem with her son but undertook a series of tactics to get her child back on track. She explains: 'Oliver was so angry all the time and I felt so guilty because I had never been with his father and I think that really damaged him. But when he was about fourteen he suddenly shot up and became much taller than me and started to boss me around. I started cowering from him and I'm sure he knew because he got worse. I did become very frightened of coming home because as soon as I got in and he would call me a bitch and a slut. Eventually I had to get help and I went to his headmaster who helped me to get a grip on Olly. I started to grab back some power by asserting myself, which isn't really my natural way. I'm quite a softy. But I could see that he was getting aggressive with me and I was losing control like he was the parent and I was the child. Eventually he started some counselling through the school and, thank God, it started to work. I went a few times with him and we sorted out some problems between us. But he didn't want to go at first and I found out he was using a lot of speed so I told him that if he didn't go for counselling I would send him to a drug centre which was residential and I think that shocked him into changing. I had to change too because I had to show my love more and not criticise him all the time. I had been afraid of having another relationship because I felt guilty that my attention was being diverted but through my own counselling I realised how one sided that was and I needed to get some balance in my life as an adult not just a mum. After a couple of rocky years we have developed a much more respectful relationship and Olly doesn't seem depressed or distracted like he once was. It's been a hard lesson but I think we'll be OK.'

It's important to be able to talk about the substances you think your child is taking. Don't be afraid. If you look up the current information (there are lots of resources at the back of this book) and become familiar with what drug is popular, you can talk openly about drugs and alcohol. You don't need to know the slang, just use the proper names for things e.g. cannabis is also known as green, dope, bud, badger, pot, hash, brown sauce. There is no point in trying to be 'cool' when talking about drugs; even when I asked my sixteen-year-old son for these slang names he gave me a wry look as if to say 'who are you kidding' and I was only asking for information! It can seem like a shady world but if you talk about it, it brings the subject out into the light and there's less space for the teenager to hide. Once dialogue takes place you can also talk about the consequences both physically and legally. Arm yourself with all the appropriate information before you start and ensure you have a 'tough love' strategy in place if you think it necessary.

Once you have started to talk to your child, be specific. Don't make sweeping statements. Talk about the specific aspects of their drug use that you think are a problem. Be direct. Talk about how their behaviour affects you or the rest of the family. At the same time, be calm. Easier said than done of course, but try not to shout or let the discussion become an argument. Better to leave it and return to it later.

But be open. Listen to what your child has to say. Write it down if it helps and consider it later. Don't react to bad language or shocking stories. Just stay neutral and keep it broad. Don't just focus on the drug use or your child's behaviour, look at the wider context and your list of possible reasons your child is using drugs.

If you feel that you are not ready for this face-to-face conversation, ask someone else to do it. There maybe a good teacher, school counsellor or family friend who would have the confidence to tackle such a subject with your child without them seeing it as a betrayal or as opting out. Make sure your child also has access to all the facts, that they know the relevant website addresses, phone numbers of helplines etc.

It's a long process. You can't expect to get everything sorted in one conversation, but it's a start. Acknowledging what the issues are is the first step towards solving them. In my experience of family members using drugs and drinking to excess when the consequences have become too great to ignore, and the whole family has been involved in an intervention, it's actually a liberating experience. If substance abuse has been taking place then a lot of denial, covering up, ignoring, disbelieving and badly informed conduct has been taking place and this is not a healthy environment. Therefore when the abuse is confronted, so are a whole host of other behaviours, habits and thinking. The experience can be used to sweep across the board and it may be painful but also positively life changing.

If you have ever sat in Al-Anon (a 12-Step group for families of alcoholics) or Families Anonymous (a 12-Step group for families of addicts) rooms where people talk about their children's 'drinking' you will often hear the statement 'Thank God for my child's drinking problem or I would never have had a chance to sort my life out.' And this approach to your child's depression could change many things in your life for the better.

One final thing, whatever else you say, the most immediate message children need repeated is that if they have been drinking or using drugs, they must not drive a car and if they know of someone else who has been drinking or using drugs, they must not get into their car. Let them know that there will be no criticism from you if they have to call you up at night for help in getting home. Thousands of parents know the pain of this tragedy.

Stealing

When a child steals it can feel devastating and parents are naturally concerned. But stealing can be a sign of a depression and the child may be stealing, not because they are turning into a juvenile delinquent, but because they feel an emotional dearth in their lives. A child who does not have his emotional needs met feels empty inside. He may take things in an attempt to fill the void. Many children do not get the attention they need. Such a child may feel unloved or that the parents are not interested in him. Often children who steal are lonely or having trouble in school or with friends. Because they lack the tools or the opportunity to express their feelings, they 'act them out' instead.

A five-year-old child, or under, may take something which excites his or her interest. This isn't stealing because the child has not fully grasped that taking something which belongs to another person is wrong. As parents we would actively teach our children about property and the consideration of others. But our behaviour is a teaching tool for our children and if we come home with stationery or pens from the office or celebrate the mistake that the checkout girl made at the supermarket which has given you a 'free gift' then our lessons about honesty will be a lot harder for our child to understand.

Although they know that theft is wrong, older children or teenagers steal for various reasons. A youngster may steal to make things equal if a brother or sister seems to be favoured with affection or gifts. Sometimes, a child may steal to give out gifts to try to buy friendships and to be more

accepted by peers. However, some children steal out of a
fear of dependency; they don't want to depend on anyone,
so they take what they need and needy children become
greedy children. I was very needy when I was a child and I
took things that weren't mine because it felt like a present to
myself and it was the only thing to make myself feel better.
Although I knew it was wrong, my neediness was greater
than my moral.

Your child may steal out of a need for more attention. Or
the child may be expressing anger or trying to 'get even' with
his or her parents; the stolen object may become a substitute
for love or affection. Whatever the reason for stealing, and
it may be that you never get to the bottom of it because
children cannot articulate their motivations like adults, your
best recourse is twofold.

What to do if your child is stealing

Firstly, you have to deal with the morality of stealing and to
do this you can do one or more of the following:

- ✸ Explain to the child that stealing is wrong
- ✸ Help the child to pay for or return the stolen object; the
  embarrassment of taking the object back to the shop or
  owner will be a life lesson
- ✸ Make sure that the child does not benefit from the theft
  in any way
- ✸ But once the item is returned and reprimand duly
  delivered, avoid lecturing the child and don't consider
  the child to be a thief or a bad person
- ✸ Make clear that this behaviour is totally unacceptable
  within the family and the community

Once the child has paid for or returned the stolen
merchandise, the parents should not bring the matter up
again, so that the child can begin again with a 'clean slate'.

Secondly, it is important that you make an effort to give more recognition to the child as an important family member. This is dealt with more fully in Chapter 3 under 'Nurturing the Soul', which discusses the importance of changing the family focus to be child centred, which will help your child overcome depression. Children who repeatedly steal may have difficulty trusting others and forming close relationships. This is why the family unit is so vital for the emotional health of the child (see Chapter 4 'The Family Affair'), because if trust is developed between the family members in most cases the stealing stops.

Violence

A child's violence can range from a passing phase of school bullying to full-blown domestic violence and anything in between. You will have signs of violence if it is taking place out of the house. These can be consistent loss of temper, frequent physical fighting, an increase in risk-taking behaviour, announcing threats or plans for hurting others or enjoying hurting animals.

How does a child with depression become violent? Violence is an outward expression of anger and/or rage. Rage is born out of a frustration when something precious is taken away. Whatever has been lost has to have been very precious to the child for him to be acting out his rage in a violent way. The most devastating loss a child could have is the loss of his dignity. When dignity has been taken away it can feel like there is nothing left for the child to reach for and all that remains is the fury to which he is entitled. Some reasons for a child to become violent could be family violence or emotional cruelty.

A study focused on 256 families who were referred to the projects after their behaviour had resulted in them being threatened by eviction and homelessness. The study showed that 59 of the families suffered from depression and a further 21 per cent were affected by other mental health problems. High levels of family violence were also reported and the children referred to the project had a high incidence of behavioural problems, with almost one in five being diagnosed with ADHD, as compared to three to eight per cent of school-age children in the general population.[24]

Amazingly, parents still believe in smacking children and Raising Kids produced a survey in October 2006 which revealed that a third of parents still smack their children, with 73 per cent saying that they felt good behaviour is more important than making children feel good about themselves. All of us want to be around children who are considerate, well behaved and who respect others, but physical punishment does not instil these values. Dr Pat Spungin, founder of Raising Kids, said, 'Children who are frequently hit are more aggressive, and more prone to developing emotional and mental health problems, particularly depression.'

There are some common themes that run through children who are violent. These include shutting off their feelings and not registering any empathy for others. In turn, their lack of remorse serves to worsen the problem. They often have distorted thinking and believe that overpowering another is a show of strength and the right way to sort out an argument. Low self-esteem is usually at the centre of a violent child's emotional health and this is backed up by feelings of victimisation, even if it is they who are being violent because they see it as a way of defending their own place in the world. And finally, they never feel safe and always feel that the world is against them.

---

24 'Anti Social Behaviour Intensive Family Support Projects 2006' from the Centre for Education Research and Social Inclusion at Sheffield Hallam University

Dealing with a violent child

Although it isn't difficult to recognise many of these beliefs and emotions in children who act violently, it can be hard to know how to correct them. While it is clear to the outside that many of the ideas the violent child harbours are wrong and that the scope of his feelings is questionable, from the inside, these thoughts and feelings make perfect sense. Every experience the child has seems to reinforce the idea that the world is a hostile, uncaring place.

In order for the depressed child to stop acting out his distress through violence, it is necessary to build a strong bond with the child so he can recover some of his lost innocence and naivety, which has taken him to a place where he has to lash out to protect his very being. You have to bear in mind that a violent child has to justify his actions to such a degree that he is blind to the rights and wrongs. In one sense you have to begin at the beginning and search for the 'lost' child inside that body which seems so aggressive. As with all other areas of depression, the starting point for helping a violent child is unconditional love and regard, even if it seems the hardest thing to do, because this is what the child needs to build a bridge back to wholeness.

So the approach to helping a child who is violent and depressed is two pronged. One is to address their behaviour. Children must be taught the wrongs of hurting another person and this subject can range widely. There are many great resources and organisations that deal with this issue. There are some relevant resources at the end of this book that offer encouraging guidance. And two is to step into the child's world and try to grasp the centre of his pain which may explain why he acting it out through aggression.

Eating Disorders

Eating disorders can be strongly linked to depression, especially in girls. There are three major types of eating disorders:

Anorexia Nervosa

Children with anorexia nervosa have a distorted body image that causes them to see themselves as overweight even when they're dangerously thin. Often refusing to eat, exercising compulsively and developing unusual habits such as refusing to eat in front of others, they lose large amounts of weight and, in the worst case, may even starve to death.

Bulimia Nervosa

Children with bulimia nervosa eat excessive quantities of food, then purge their bodies of the food and calories they fear by using laxatives, enemas or diuretics, vomiting and/or exercising. Often acting in secrecy, they feel disgusted and ashamed as they binge, yet relieved of tension and negative emotions once their stomachs are empty again.

Binge eating

Like children with bulimia, those with binge-eating disorder experience frequent episodes of out-of-control eating. The difference is that binge eaters don't rid their bodies of excess calories.

Eating disorders are associated with emotional disorders like depression. Researchers don't yet know whether eating disorders are symptoms of such problems or whether the problems develop because of the isolation, stigma and physiological changes wrought by the eating disorders themselves. What is clear is that people with eating disorders suffer higher rates of depression, anxiety disorders and substance abuse than other people.

In our highly body-conscious society, which continues to prize thinness even as Britons become heavier than ever before, it is no wonder that almost everyone worries about their weight at least occasionally. People with eating disorders take such concerns to extremes, developing abnormal eating habits that threaten their wellbeing and even their lives.

It's important to prevent problematic behaviours from evolving into full-fledged eating disorders. Anorexia and bulimia, for example, are usually preceded by very strict dieting and weight loss. Binge-eating disorder can begin with occasional binging. Whenever eating behaviours start having a destructive impact on someone's functioning or self-image, it's time to see a highly trained mental health professional, such as a psychologist trained and experienced in treating people with eating disorders.

Who suffers from eating disorders?

According to the National Institute of Mental Health, adolescents and young women account for 90 per cent of cases. But eating disorders aren't just a problem for the teenage girls so often depicted in the media.

People sometimes have eating disorders without their families or friends ever suspecting that they have a problem. Aware that their behaviour is abnormal, people with eating disorders may withdraw from social contact, hide their behaviour and deny that their eating patterns are problematic. Making an accurate diagnosis may require the involvement of an appropriate mental health expert.

What causes eating disorders?

Certain psychological factors predispose people to developing eating disorders. Troubled families or relationships are one factor. Personality traits also may contribute to these disorders. Most people with eating disorders suffer from low self-esteem, feelings of helplessness and intense dissatisfaction with the way they look. Specific traits are linked to each of the disorders. People with anorexia tend to be perfectionists, for instance, and are trying to mask their depression, while people with bulimia are often impulsive and want to be rid of depressed feelings and therefore purge their bodies.

Why is it important to seek treatment for these disorders?

Research indicates that eating disorders are one of the psychological problems least likely to be treated. But eating disorders often don't go away on their own. And leaving them untreated can have serious consequences. It's a horrible fact that the National Institute of Mental Health estimates that one in ten anorexia cases ends in death from starvation, suicide or medical complications like heart attacks or kidney failure. However, there are a number of places you can turn to for help.

Who can help?

The good news is that most cases of eating disorder can be treated successfully by appropriately trained health and mental health care professionals. Treatments do not work instantly and for some patients the treatment may need to be long term.

For parents unable to cope with a child's eating disorder, turning to a psychologist with an expertise in food disorders may be appropriate. Psychologists play a vital role in the successful treatment of eating disorders and are integral members of the multidisciplinary team that may be required to provide care for your child. As part of this treatment, a doctor may be called on to rule out medical illnesses and determine that the patient is not in immediate physical danger. A nutritionist may be asked to help assess and improve nutritional intake. There are also support and self-help groups, and personal and telephone counselling services that can help.

Once the psychologist has identified important issues that need attention and developed a treatment plan, he or she helps the patient replace destructive thoughts and behaviours with more positive ones. A psychologist and patient might work together to focus on health rather than weight, for example. Or a patient might keep a food diary as a way of becoming more aware of the types of situations that trigger bingeing.

Incorporating family therapy into patient care could be a big help to prevent relapses by resolving family issues related to the eating disorder. Therapists can guide family members in understanding the patient's disorder and learning new techniques for coping with problems. Support groups can also help. Remember: the sooner treatment starts the better. The longer abnormal eating patterns continue, the more deeply ingrained they become and the more difficult they are to treat.

While you may get help from the professionals, the way to help your child at home is to love him as you love yourself. Your child maybe a teenager now but that doesn't mean he is averse to some parental cherishment and nourishment, a cuddle on the sofa or a shared moment having some fun. Teenagers struggle for their independence and although they may appear rejecting of their parents, they desperately need to know that their parents' love is as strong as ever.

There are no easy answers but one final suggestion is to trust your child. Teenagers with eating disorders tend to feel inadequate but by encouraging their initiative and

independence you can support their autonomy, which will
enforce that you trust them, and this may help them recover
from depression as well.

Low self-esteem

What lies behind us and what lies before us are tiny matters
compared to what lies within us.

Ralph Waldo Emerson, writer

Most people feel bad about themselves at sometime.
Feelings of low self-esteem may be triggered by being treated
poorly by someone else recently or in the past, or by a
person's own judgements of him or herself. This is normal.
However, low self-esteem is usually a constant companion
for a depressed child. The peak age of depression correlates
with the peak years of low self-esteem, which is early and
middle adolescence,[25] with a peak period between the ages
of thirteen and fourteen. At this point children will feel bad
about themselves and this will keep them from feeling happy
and fully alive.

Symptoms of low self-esteem:

❋ avoiding trying new things
❋ feeling unloved and unwanted
❋ blaming others for his own shortcomings
❋ feeling, or pretending to feel, emotionally indifferent
❋ being unable to tolerate a normal level of frustration
❋ putting down his own talents and abilities
❋ being easily influenced

Low self-esteem *always* forms in childhood when a child is
developing his initial view of himself and his attributes and

---

25 S. Feldman and G. Elliott, 'Adolescence: path to a productive life or a
diminished future?', *Carnegie Quarterly*, 35 (1990), 1–13

depression, in many children, is actually a symptom of low self-esteem.

Studies have shown that low self-esteem and depression often go hand in hand. In fact the World Health Organisation (WHO) uses low self-esteem and self-worth in its description of depression. Low self-esteem makes you your own worst enemy. Thoughts of 'if only I were prettier', 'if only I was good at sports', 'if only I was funny or popular', 'if only I was strong enough to fix this' crowd out everything else. But the low self-esteem voice inside a child's head may become so strong that even if they receive positive support they may discount it. Like Julia Roberts said in *Pretty Woman* 'the bad stuff is easier to believe'.

How to help a child with low self-esteem

It is important to nurture the child from inside the family and to change the family culture towards cherishing the child and this is covered in the next chapter. However, there are three simple approaches you can use for the child with low self-esteem:

1. Tell your child when you feel good about him.
It is easy to express negative feelings to children but somehow not get around to describing positive feelings. A child doesn't know when you are feeling good about him and he needs to hear you tell him that you like having him in the family. Children remember positive statements we say to them. They store them up like squirrels storing their nuts and 'replay' these statements to themselves. Practise giving your child encouraging words throughout each day. If this isn't a part of your family culture it is simple to start straight away.

Some words of encouragement might include:

I'm so proud to be your mum/dad
Yes
Good
You're doing great
Excellent
I love the way you do that
Good for you
That's much better
What a brilliant idea
Great behaviour today
You're the best
I'm so glad you're mine
Now you've got it

I also like to tell my children whenever someone else tells me something good about them because otherwise they don't receive the information. Have you ever been to a parents' meeting at school or a family occasion when others talk delightfully about your child but the child is excluded from the conversation? I have and it seems such a waste if the good feedback isn't given to the person to whom it's intended. I always explain that the other person was thrilled with their progress or thought them a pleasure to have around. It has taken a lot of practice to say this naturally because I was brought up to believe that whatever adults said was private and I never knew if they liked me or not. I think the ethos of the time was that good things said to the child might 'spoil' them! But praise is so sporadic but so, so rewarding to give.

2. Learn to be generous with praise – but be specific. Children like general praise but what really helps them is knowing why they received it because they come to know what is 'good' and what is 'bad' and in order to receive more praise they will be more inclined to practise the 'good'. You

can get into the habit of looking for situations in which
your child is doing a good job or displaying a talent. For
instance when your child completes a job you could say, 'I
really like the way you tidied your room. You found a place
for everything and put each thing in its place.' When you see
them showing talent you could say, 'That last Irish jig you
did was great. I couldn't possibly remember all those moves
like you did.' Don't be afraid to give praise often, even in
front of family or friends.

Again, if you never received it as a child you might
find this difficult but it's simply a matter of overcoming
your hesitancy with practice. Also, use praise to point out
individual qualities. For instance, 'You are a very kind
person.' Or, 'I like the way you get to the end of a difficult
job.' You can even praise a child for *something he did not do*
such as 'I really liked how you accepted my answer of "no"
and didn't lose your temper.' Watch him puff out as you
deliver your praise – it's almost physical.

3. Teach your child to practise making positive statements to
himself.

Self-talk rules our world. How we see the world is a direct
reflection of what we tell ourselves. Negative self-talk is
behind depression. What we think determines how we feel
and how we feel determines how we behave. Therefore, it is
important to teach children to be positive about how they
'talk to themselves'. Some examples of useful self-talk are: 'I
can do it,' 'I am a very kind boy,' or 'I am OK just the way I
am.' It may be useful to write out a few of these statements
and put them on your child's bedroom wall. Just seeing them
every day is a way of increasing his self-esteem.

And finally – avoid shaming the child:

Avoid shaming the child through criticism. Contaminated
shame is what we feel when we think we are no good as

opposed to guilt which is when we feel bad for 'doing' something that is no good. Sometimes it is necessary to criticise a child's actions and it is appropriate that parents do so. When, however, the criticism is directed to the child as a person, it can easily deteriorate into shame. It is important to criticise the action rather than the child, e.g. 'It's not OK to hit your sister if you feel angry and I do not like the hitting.' By explaining that the deed is not acceptable, this doesn't infringe on the child's core and he will learn that he has to control his actions but he is still OK as a loveable child. One good tip is always to use 'I' statements rather than 'You' statements when giving criticism. For instance, say, 'I would like you to keep your clothes in the proper place in your wardrobe or drawers not lying all over your room,' rather than saying 'You are such a lazy slob. Can't you look after anything?'

By changing a few degrees in the way you talk to your child, you can begin to turn his esteem from a negative balance to a credit balance. You will see results from the very beginning and you will be thrilled at how quickly he responds.

Chapter 3
Recovery

🖐 NURTURING YOUR CHILD TO RECOVERY

The best way to make children good is to make them happy.
Oscar Wilde

Now that you have a better understanding of the causes of childhood depression and how children will 'act out' their emotions, it's now time to take steps to nurture them to recovery. In the following chapters I have laid out a plan which will show you how you can help your child by making sure all his emotional needs are satisfied, which will give him all the tools he needs to grow into a happy, well-balanced individual.

I have broken the recovery process down into four broad areas. In 'Nurturing the Soul' I'll explain how a parent's unconditional love can provide security and an emotional safety net, which will allow your child to blossom and thrive and achieve his potential. The links between mood and food are becoming more and more apparent to us, and in 'Nourishing the Body' I'll show you how a healthy diet, full of good mood foods, along with exercise, can be a fantastic tool in fighting your child's depression. A happy child is one who has boundaries, and a lack of boundaries can be a contributing factor in a child's depression, so in 'Setting Boundaries' you'll learn how to set boundaries which will give your child a sense of security and safety. Finally, a loving and supportive team of people can really help nurture a depressed child to happiness, and this is what the section entitled 'Building the Team' is all about.

⊕ NURTURING THE SOUL

How a child is nurtured can determine his emotional well-being for the rest of his life. If he is cherished with passion and commitment, fairness and respect he will grow into a steady, happy adult with a high degree of satisfaction in being the person he is.

For myself, I have to admit that I have not always found it easy to nurture my children. I do know, however, that my ability to nurture my children is directly linked with how I nurture myself. If I'm happy then I am completely available to my children and I'm able to love them up, step into their world and be passionate about how their life is going. If I'm not feeling so good then this will slip. It's a very complicated business and it's tricky to know exactly where to start because we, as parents, can only give as good as we feel.

Sometimes it's hard to know if our children are being nurtured and there's no point in asking them because they cannot answer the question as everything they receive they perceive as 'normal'. Let's simplify this by taking a quick look at the rights of a child.

A child has the right...
* To be fed with nourishing food and watered
* To be safe, warm, sheltered and secure
* To be touched, held and caressed
* To be loved without any conditions attached
* To be respected as a unique human being regardless of our behaviour
* To be able to make mistakes
* To ask for what they need
* To say they don't understand
* To change their minds

✳ To decline responsibility for another's problems
✳ To express their feelings
✳ To be happy

These are the essentials that are necessary to nurture the child. They are the basics that all of us need to grow into fully developed, happy adults. These rights may be obvious, they are certainly profound, but they are right on track with what the well-known psychologists such as Maslow and Rogers would agree with. In order to fully function and blossom into self-actualisation, these are the basic rights that need to be met.

Maslow's Hierarchy of Needs

Abraham Maslow was a psychologist born in 1908 in New York. He devised what has become known as Maslow's Hierarchy of Needs. Here is a diagram explaining it:

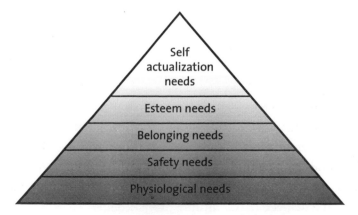

At the bottom of the pyramid are our physiological needs – air, water, food, shelter and sleep. The second layer contains safety and security needs – a sense of security in a predictable world with a relative absence of threat to ourselves. The third layer designates love and belongingness needs – warm, interpersonal sharing, love and affection. The fourth layer designates self-esteem and regard by others – a sense of confidence and competence, achievement, independence and freedom. At the top of the pyramid are self-actualisation needs – growth, development, realising potential and becoming the best that we are capable of.

This illustration serves to sum up what we need as humans to feel fully alive. Assuming all these are in place, the probability is that we will feel happy and depression will not be a part of our life.

Unconditional Love

Before you were conceived I wanted you
Before you were born I loved you
Before you were here an hour I would die for you
This is the miracle of life.

Maureen Hawkins, writer

What is unconditional love?

Love is either conditional or unconditional. In other words, there are either conditions attached to love or there are no conditions attached to love; there is no third possibility. Adult, romantic love, for example, is conditional and that is appropriate. Would you continue to love someone if they were unfaithful, verbally abusive, assaulted you etc.? Probably not, so that would be the condition. With a child, however, it is different.

Unconditional love is the love you have for a child It is the love that states 'no matter what you do or say I will always love you with every piece of my heart'. Unconditional love will surpass every single act, deed, statement, behaviour, tantrum, outburst, undertaking etc. that it is possible for the child to do. No matter what, unconditional love will see to it that the parent stands by, loves, supports and cherishes that child. If the child were to commit some terrible act, the worst act that is possible to commit, unconditional love will say 'although I hate the act of . . . that you have done, I will always love the essence of you and nothing will ever change that'.

With unconditional love you don't need to say it that often. As long as you mean it when you say it then your actions will confirm that pledge every day. With a depressed child you may choose to say it three or four times but it's really not necessary to say it any more than that because if you do you may diminish its value. The day my mother left home, when I was sixteen, her last words to me were 'Now you know I love you, don't you?' I was shocked because I had never heard her say that she loved me, I couldn't understand why she was saying it now and because I had never felt loved, the words were hollow. If I had felt loved she wouldn't have needed to say those words. It's the same with any child; the love is demonstrated and does not need to be verbally forced.

Unconditional love is a gift and it is free. There is no price a child has to pay to receive it. It means that they can say whatever they want to say, do whatever they want to do in the absolute confidence that no love will be taken away. A child does not need to be in fear of any withdrawal of love regardless of what they have done or said. They can be as honest and as open as they want and although boundaries will be set for behaviour, love will not be withdrawn – ever.

There will be times when the relationship with a child becomes rocky, when troubled waters flow under the bridge of unconditional love and when there may seem a huge distance between the parent and child but unconditional love will serve as that bridge and will never waver in the face of adversity. Unconditional love means that no matter what, the commitment is there and there will be no going back. No matter what, unconditional love is prepared to hear whatever negative thoughts need to be said and will receive them as reverently as receiving positive, warm thoughts.

Someone who has committed their unconditional love for another may not always be able to predict their reactions to what is said or done but they will never reject the loved child. They are committed to the child's happiness and growth.

What does this mean for the child?

Unconditional love for a child means that affirmation for his very soul does not depend on making the parents proud, getting good school marks or conforming to family rules. Unconditional love is required as the 'all mighty' safety net upon which the child is free to fall into at any time. It's the safety of knowing that no matter how hard a child tries and fails, he is not loved any less and he is not regarded any less.

No other relationship can sustain unconditional love like the parent/child relationship. Because the child needs the parents love to survive, if the love from the parent is conditional, the child will suppress any feelings of hurt, neglect, abuse etc. and keep the love for the parent alive and strong in order that the parent takes care of them. Suppressing these feelings leads to depression.

For a child to feel and know the gift of unconditional love, this means the child can aspire to expand himself into his full potential, knowing he has the softness of the unconditional love to fall back on and to help him, when he stumbles and drops, to stand back on his own two feet.

It's the word 'unconditional' rather than the word 'love' that makes the difference. 'Unconditional' means without conditions or reservations; it is absolute. We continue to love our children through good times and bad, and we don't stop loving them if they don't meet our expectations.

The one thing a child fears is that they have disappointed the parent. Unconditional love means never having to fear a parent's disappointment. We love our children even when we might consider them unlovable; our love doesn't stop when they have made a choice that would not have been our choice. Unconditional love transcends any other type of love.

Healing and thriving through unconditonal love

When we feel love and kindness toward others, it not only makes others feel loved and cared for, but it helps us also to develop inner happiness and peace.

HH The Dalai Lama

When I first read about unconditional love and the philosophy behind it, I felt slightly queasy. 'Unconditional love' seemed too soppy, drippy and wet. I certainly never discussed it with anyone and decided the whole notion was for wimps! However, as I have 'grown up' I have come to realise that the reason I felt repelled by the idea was that I never received it and therefore never had that profound understanding of the idea that anyone could have that high regard for me.

It was when my first son was born that I had to reassess these values and what I learned was that every child is entitled to the profoundness of unconditional love and, in spite of myself, I had the potential to feel it for my son. What I had to tackle was my own cynicism and defence. That was broken down after acknowledging the huge gulf between what I felt for my son and what I had never received as a child. It seemed that we were entangled in some way, that I couldn't separate my own feelings of deficiency with my son who was obviously loved. To clarify this: I looked at my son and thought he was deficient but I was simply projecting my own neediness onto him.

It took a lot of self-growth to turn this round to see that he and I were different. Along the way I accepted that unconditional love was one way and that a child's love for the parent is based on the need to survive but the parental love for the child is not based on anything. The journey was painful but worth it, because it gave me the opportunity to completely heal myself of any childhood deficiency. What a priceless gift.

Healing takes place when a parent offers a child the gift of unconditional love. There is nothing else that can heal the human soul more than love that has no conditions. In offering a child your unconditional love you are offering yourself as a source of wisdom and guidance that the child can learn to rely on so that he can build a new arena from where he can build a bridge to the outside world.

We have been deluded in thinking that criticisms, punishments and keeping them *in line* are the means by which to stimulate and motivate a child to grow into a happy human being. This approach only serves to create a defended child, one who has to monitor his existence and to shape himself to adhere to the rules. This doesn't feed the divinity of the child; but unconditional love does.

A child is like a small plant. If the child is depressed it will struggle in the soil, wilting and waiflike. Unconditional love is your care. If you nourish the plant with enough water and plant food, flood it with warm sunshine, place it under cover when the storm comes, and keep away the bugs that try to eat it, you will see the plant grow strong and tall, unfurl into its own glory, open its buds give you the joy of its blossoms and scent.

Once a child has learned to trust that the love is there, and this may involve some trial and error on his part, he will begin to heal the shattered parts of himself, becoming whole again. With this wholeness will come new knowledge; the knowledge of himself. He will learn where his limits are, having been put in place by his parents and he will respect that. He will feel free to experiment and when he falls he will feel supported. But the progression will give him courage, raise his self-esteem, his self-trust and create an abundant world in which he can laugh, play and feel ready to work.

Keeping the invisible energy *low*

The great omission in American life is solitude ... that zone of time and space, free from the outside pressures, which is the incinerator of the spirit.

Marya Mannes, writer

What is the 'invisible' energy? It is the energy created by modern life: the internet, informational overload, media indoctrination, computer and console games, television etc., which stimulate and excite children. The stimulus is such that more traditional ways of self-entertaining can seem 'boring' e.g. riding a bike, playing football with friends, drawing and painting etc. It's as if the modern invention brings an invisible energy into the house and we only know about it when the children are highly charged or worn out but they don't seem to have done anything.

Believe it or not, there are now treatment centres to assist children with computer game addiction in the same way that drug addiction is managed. When time spent on the computer, playing console games or cruising the internet reaches a point that it harms a child's or adult's family and social relationships, or disrupts school or work life, that person may be caught in a cycle of addiction.

Like other addictions, the computer or console game has replaced friends and family as the source of a person's emotional life. Increasingly, to feel good, the addicted person spends more time playing video games or searching the internet. Time away from the computer or game causes moodiness or withdrawal. If the child isn't 'addicted' to these, overuse of these electronics will certainly hinder his self-resilience.

Earth the energy

The energy that works best is the energy from the earth – from the ground up. Earth energy is solid, whole and nurturing as opposed to the high energy of man-made stimulants. Think of the way the earth wire works in an electrical plug; the earth wire gives a safe route for the electrical current if the live wire touches the outer casing. In the same sense, grounding the child's energy is a way of releasing his emotional energy in a safe and positive way. We know that meditation helps depression and meditation is about grounding and linking with the calmness of the earth's energy. In modern social psychology, we know that Neuro Linguistic Programming (NLP) and other such programmes ask us to visualise going down steps, counting down from 100 to 1 and taking our consciousness from our head down to our feet. There are thousands of years of spiritual teachings devoted to this way of thinking and the benefits are documented as powerful stimuli for wellbeing.

So to keep our children's focus calm, creative, in the moment and away from distractions, we can limit the amount of time they use electronic entertainment. And in turn, we can stimulate the child's creative focal energy towards other types of entertainment.

Have you been to a house where the children have a whole room of toys devoted to them yet they are 'bored'? In one sense we have lost trust that they will actually entertain themselves if they are bored enough. Yes, we may have to go through the complaints: 'I'm fed up' 'I've got nothing to do' 'I'm so bored' but they do pass and, lo and behold, they will become interested in something else.

With older kids it's just as easy to get them focused on low-energy things to do. Getting outside is a good way to start. If you have a garden then get them working in it and, in spite of their complaints, they will love the satisfaction of clearing, digging, planting, watering, mowing etc. It's worth pointing out to them how much 'everyone' enjoyed getting the garden straight by enhancing the positive side to the activity. If you have no garden then straightening out a room in the house can be immensely satisfying.

It may be that only having the television on at certain times works well in the family. Replacing some television time with some family fun at the weekend can be a good start. Children tend to feel happier if they are supported by their parents and it may take a little encouragement for everyone, including parents, to get the cards out but making time for interactive fun like this really works to help bring a child out of a depressive state.

Bringing the energy down from a super-heightened, unnatural state to a more ecological, unprocessed spirit can calm the home environment and limit the opportunities for modern toxicity to creep in and contaminate the children. Undeniably, there will be a marked difference in the child's behaviour as research (National Institute on Media & the Family, National Summit on Video Games, Youth & Public Policy, October 2006) shows that high-energy entertainment such as PC games can have a 'devastating' effect on children. By introducing a more controlled environment you can have better control on what's influencing your children.

Listening with love

There is nothing that makes a child feel more cared about than to be listened to. Take the time to be with your child as an interested, non-judgemental friend, and listen to what he has to say. Listen with respect. Children's concerns may be different from ours, but the emotions they feel are the same. Give your child freedom to express his feelings and views without fear of ridicule or judgement. Show him that you acknowledge and respect what he has to say.

Listening sets early patterns for life-long communication skills. If you take the time to listen, you teach them they are important. You help them trust their own perceptions. You also improve communication and make it easier to talk to them in the future. 'Listening time' pays off in trust and courtesy down the road.

Children view 'listening' as the best support they can receive and research has shown that children who have abundant parental support are less likely to suffer from depression.[26]

It is very hard but vitally important to listen to your child, even when you don't like what you are hearing, and to repeat back what you heard to make sure you understood him correctly. Sometimes we don't like what we hear, especially if it is said in an angry, loud or disrespectful way but this is a gift because the child is trusting you with the truth. At these times it's important to listen and reflect back the child's feelings. You can say, 'I hear you are upset about not being able to go to the beach today.' This helps your child further explore his feelings and actions, and lets him know you are listening to him and understand the feelings he is having.

---

26 *Psychology and Aging,* March 2004, a journal published by the American Psychological Association

Later, when the child has calmed down, you can talk to him about ways in which he can let you know he is angry without screaming, or yelling, or being disrespectful.

The practice of good communication skills is not always easy, but with practise it does get easier and can soon become a normal communicating tool. And it is the one way you can be fully present and available for your child, which is the most powerful means with which you can help your child.

Teach your child to trust themselves

People take different roads seeking fulfilment and happiness. Just because they're not on your road doesn't mean they've gotten lost.

H. Jackson Brown Jr, writer

To teach children to trust themselves is a skill that can make the difference between getting *through* life and getting *from* life. As a child I didn't trust myself and my feelings; I always thought I was wrong and I couldn't protect myself from the harshness of the world. I was constantly bullied and responded with aggression, which alienated me from others. I can only imagine how different my life might have been if I could assess my feelings and my life with measure and assurance. It's for this reason more than any other I love to teach my children to trust themselves.

Listen
It starts with the simple task of listening as we discussed above. Listening says to the child, *what you say is important to me and I will stop everything else to be still and to hear you.* That in itself is an endorsement of his essence; that you truly believe he is worthy of your time. Children learn by copying and he will learn that he is important through your listening.

He will feel important to himself, that he is worthy of an adult's attention. This in itself will increase his esteem.

Mirror

By mirroring his feelings he has the opportunity to cement his own trust because he knows you have heard him. When you mirror, you reflect back what he said to you (no matter how painful or uncomfortable it is for you) and, if you have to, word for word. He can do two things: correct you if he thinks you didn't quite hear it correctly and reflect on what he's hearing from you and correct himself if he didn't get it quite right. He has the opportunity to clarify what he has said.

Acknowledge

By you acknowledging his feelings he can take the opportunity to endorse the truth for himself. For example, if he says he was very frightened of the dog, you can acknowledge that by saying 'Yes, I understand why you felt frightened of the dog because dogs can be very scary'; if the older child is in trouble for skipping a class at school and he explained that he was scared because he hadn't finished his homework, you can acknowledge this by saying 'I can understand why you didn't get to the class if you were scared of getting into trouble.' By accepting and acknowledging a child's feelings it is possible to bond through mutual trust and acceptance – a real gift for both parent and child.

Love with evidence

How often do we get an opportunity to receive really good, trustworthy information about ourselves? It hardly ever happens, yet it is one of the most liberating and nurturing things we can offer another person. By this I mean just that – evidence of what it is about your child that you love. For example, 'I loved it when you helped your friends in the swimming pool. You know you are a better swimmer but you swam slowly so they could play next to you.' Or 'I love the fact that you really enjoyed mowing the lawn and clearing up afterwards because it shows you are diligent and thorough and those are two great skills.'

When you give love with evidence you are backing up your 'I love you' statements and they are undeniable. If you offer evidence no child can argue because you have the proof. I promise if you try this you will see them immediately puff out with pride!

Teach them to get a perspective

Children get very caught up in childhood politics very quickly and a depressed child can come off badly because they are vulnerable. The rough and tumble of childhood might be a little severe sometimes and it's important for them to get a perspective, or a little objectivity, to get them through the day. Here are two good tips to help them:

1. Reading the forehead

You can often sum up another person by imagining a 'strap line' written on their forehead. Their demeanour, mood and the way they present themselves will give enough clues as to how they present themselves. When dealing with adults you can suggest to a child that they look at the adult's forehead and stab a guess at what the invisible writing says. The results can be very revealing. I have heard such things as:

> 'Smile for the camera?'
> 'I hate kids.'
> 'Get me out of here.'
> 'Be nice to me, please.'
> 'I have to talk to you but I don't want to!'

2. Brush it off
When dealing with other children, if something has been said to the child and it has left them feeling bad, they are to brush it off their shoulders like it's a little bit of dandruff. It's a great feeling; I do it all the time with others' remarks and it's so satisfying. Just get rid of whatever verbal debris was left behind.

Good perception

Once some of these techniques filter through into the child and they begin to feel better, you can start to help them assess their place in the world.

Good perception can be a great asset for any child but especially one who is feeling a little down on himself. When someone is depressed, they see the world through a pessimistic veil and it can be very hard for them to receive feedback without always seeing it as negative.

Children who can accurately assess how people feel about them, even if those feelings are negative, are less likely to show symptoms of depression, according to Florida State University researchers. Psychology Professor Janet Kistner says, 'Our results support the perspective that realistic perceptions are a hallmark of mental health.' This is a significant statement because it shows that accuracy is the key and not whether children thought that other children liked them or not. That's important because some psychologists have theorised that people who have a positive bias, meaning they think others like them more than they actually do, are protected against developing symptoms of depression, while those who have a negative bias are prone to maladjustment and depression. The researchers found neither to be true. What they were able to establish, however, was that greater social acceptance is associated with fewer symptoms of depression.

Therefore, through the mirroring and acknowledgement concepts, it is possible to help a child to gauge his relationships with his peers and establish how they are viewed ensuring that, through evidence, a child's view of themselves can be determined. If a child says their friend 'doesn't like me any more', you can then establish why they don't and help the child to see either that it is their friend's problem and not theirs or how they could resolve the dispute to help them feel better about this friendship. By helping a child resolve problems with friends, you are expanding their emotional capabilities. Starting this at a young age (primary school onwards) can help a child really establish their own self-sufficiency and this will help build confidence.

Plan without goals

The prime purpose of being four is to enjoy being four – of secondary importance is to prepare for being five.

Jim Trelease, *The Read-Aloud Handbook*, 1985

What does that mean? Aren't we all supposed to be goal driven, attaining heady heights to stay ahead of the game? No, not really. A study has shown that conditional goal setting has been identified as a significant factor in the development and maintenance of depression in adults.[27] This study examines these same concepts among children and has found the very same thing to be true.

Planning without goals is a radical approach to life but it can prise us away from the high-pressured, Western lifestyle that insists we incessantly strive to attain goals.

---

27 'Understanding the relationships between well-being, goal-setting and depression in children', *Australian and New Zealand Journal of Psychiatry*, 38:3 (March 2004), 155, doi:10.1111/j.1440-1614.2004.01317.x

From the moment we are born we are measured, weighed and watched. My second son didn't reach crawling, talking and walking in the allotted centile and was promptly sent for evaluation where he was prodded and monitored until he reached the goals that had been set for him. It turned out he was simply slower than the line predicted he *should* have been. This taught me about goal setting and how it could be very restrictive and I know if I bow to pressure I will cause him to fret. Once children reach school they are scrutinised, badged and labelled, educationally and socially. If they swerve out of the middle centile, they may be seen as *problem* kids.

Once they reach SATS, GCSEs, AS levels and A levels, school just seems to be all about hitting goals. More and more parents are looking for an alternative style of teaching for their children. Steiner schools are a case in point. Steiner education's philosophy respects the essential nature of childhood and enables each pupil to develop the abilities and confidence needed for life as well as academic progress. The curriculum is based on a pedagogical philosophy that places emphasis on the whole development of the child, including a child's spiritual, physical and moral wellbeing.

Teaching a child to learn the inherent value of planning without goals is a gift, which will nourish them for the rest of their life. Planning without goals helps us to have a framework for the future but no goals on which to focus. This way of living can bring us more contentment, simplicity and enjoyment. It releases us from the longings and yearnings for that over which we have no control. Children are naturally brilliant at planning without goals and it is us who can learn from them. The only goals that get in their way are the ones we set for them.

Planning without goals will feed the child's sensation of being rather than doing. When we 'do' we can forget the essence of 'being'. By planning without goals, you can help him look at the 'big picture' of his life and teach him that happiness comes from being himself and in the moment rather than worrying about how he might not achieve the goals that are set in the future. We cannot control a child but we can influence him. Nurturing your child's spirituality will influence him into feeling better about himself, his place in the world and the people around him.

One way of helping your child to plan without goals is to ask him to plan how he would like the next week, month, year to turn out and to write it on a piece of paper. Once he has done it, ask him to give you the paper for safe keeping. Then ask him to sit still and imagine the paper with the plans listed on it lying on the beach next to the ocean as the waves gently wash over it. As the ink fades away into the sea foam, the paper is washed out to sea. Let him dwell in the moment – a moment of peace and stillness with no expectations or goals to worry about, just a plan.

☂ NOURISHING THE BODY

Good Mood Food

One of the very nicest things about life is the way we must regularly stop whatever it is we are doing and devote our attention to eating.

Luciano Pavarotti, singer

Good mood food is such a great way to begin to help depressed children. Food? Yes, the food we eat really affects the way we feel. Although this is a relatively new field, there is an increasing amount of research pointing towards food as having a powerful effect on the way we feel, both physically and emotionally. Even though there aren't a lot of absolutes, there is a certainty that if you eat the right food at the right time your chemistry will be balanced, which will make you feel great; eat the wrong foods at the wrong time and this may cause depression. A recent survey, carried out by the Mood and Food project run by MIND, said that of 200 people 88 per cent found that changing their diet for the better significantly improved their mood.

Of course there are many other factors that can affect the way our children feel but the exciting thing about the food/mood link is that it is something we can get started on straight away, knowing that the positive difference in how this makes a child feel can be implemented immediately. And, it's good to be able to tackle the food issue, even if it is to simply eliminate the possibility of their diet making them depressed.

The nutritional information about food is so well documented and easily available that we can actually plan meals to precisely affect how we want our children to feel. For example, if we want them to feel full of energy, we might feed them some chick peas, which are a great source of protein; if they need stamina to make them last the whole morning until lunch then a large bowl of porridge will do the trick; if they need a direct mood boost then some tuna fish could help lift their spirits with its supply of omega 3 oils. And, contrary to popular belief, foods that produce good moods can also be delicious.

Sometimes it's hard to climb out of the food habits to which the whole family has become accustomed and it can seem more bother than it's worth because of all the complaining the children are going to come up with when you suggest a 'lentil bake'! There are two concepts to start a new regime with: 'Five-a-Day' and 'Three-a-Day'. Simply focusing on these two areas will help get a more standardised eating pattern for everyone. Why for everyone? Well, it would be unhelpful to single out the depressed child for a specific food programme because they may feel like they are being isolated so it's recommended that everyone gets into new habits. But the benefits will mean that everyone feels better!

Five-a-Day

One recommendation for helping our children to boost their mood is to implement the 'Five-a-Day' rule. Scientific studies from the World Health Organisation and the Department of Health, as well as many others, recommend eating a minimum of five portions of fruit and vegetables a day. Yes, how obvious is it? But even the most conscientious parents struggle to get the five into their children every day.

A portion is approximately how much the child can hold in his hand. If your child is aged four to six, he will benefit from the School Fruit and Vegetable Scheme, which is part of the Five-a-Day programme to increase fruit and vegetable consumption. Under the scheme, all four to six year olds in local education authority maintained infant, primary and special schools are entitled to a free piece of fruit or vegetable each school day. So for younger children that's one portion taken care of.

Fruits and vegetables help to protect us from illnesses that take time to develop. What we eat now will affect our health in twenty years' time – the time taken for some illnesses, such as heart disease and cancer, to develop.

It's a double-edged sword: our immune system is lowered by chronic stress, which is a symptom of depression; but continued suppression of the immune system can lead to illness; people who are ill are more likely to feel lethargic and debilitated; lethargy and debilitation can lead to depression.

By way of contrast, happy people make for healthy

people. One study has shown that feeling good reduces the risk of disease. 'There's a direct link between how we're feeling and the biological processes that relate to illness and illness risk,' said study author Dr Andrew Steptoe, the British Heart Foundation professor of psychology at University College London. 'Biology is going to be on the side of those people who are going to be in a more positive state of mind, and it may well stand these people in good stead for their future health.'

Here are some tips for helping your children to eat their Five-a-Day and a healthy, balanced diet.

Work with what they like to eat

✳ Children like crunchy and sweet foods. So try them out on crunchy raw carrots or peppers as a snack.
✳ Add fruit and vegetables to their favourite foods, such as pizzas or sandwiches.
✳ Give them fresh fruit juice to help them get their five-a-day. But be careful – too much fruit juice can damage their teeth.

Set a good example

✳ Eat lots of fruit and vegetables yourself. Your children learn habits by watching you, so if you eat healthily, the chances are your children will too.
✳ Be consistent. Set standard meal and snack times and discourage other snacking. If your kids insist on a snack, encourage them to wait till their next meal.
✳ Don't reward your children with food – they'll remember that later on in life!

Keep trying them out on new things

✳ Try to serve several fruit and vegetable options – kids like to choose and so let them choose between good things.

✳ They may not like a particular fruit or vegetable at first, but serve it again a few days later. Encourage children to have tiny tastes each time. Research shows that tiny tastes can help children to change their taste preferences.

✳ Don't force children to eat things – this will only create negative associations and discourage them from trying again in the future.

Make it fun

✳ Make fruit and vegetables into faces on their plates, or cut them into funky shapes.

✳ Turn it into a game or challenge. You can motivate your children by giving them activity sheets or wall charts to record what fruit or vegetables they eat.

✳ Get your children involved in the cooking if you can. Let them choose recipes to try and ask them to help pick fruit and vegetables at the supermarket. They're more likely to try things they've had a hand in preparing.

Make a fruit salad

A home-made fruit salad is simple and can take just ten minutes to prepare. You can chop fruit and then add a tin of fruit in its own juice; this will give it some liquid and stop the apples going brown. Alternatively, buy a pack of mixed dried fruit from your local health store and soak in water overnight. A fruit salad makes a great breakfast, a snack for when the children get in from school – starving! – and a great pudding. Notice how good they feel after eating it – and one portion of fruit salad can count as two portions of their five-a-day. It can last up to three days and you can use seasonal fruit.

Three-a-Day

Three-a-Day refers to three meals a day. When a child is depressed or anxious, grazing through the day can become a habit that will encourage children to eat the high fat/salt/sugar foods as a comfort and, in the long run, will make them feel even more depressed. It's an easy habit to fall into and they so easily lose the habit of regularity in their food. Adopting the Three-A-Day habit is a great way to bring back some stability, consistency and good order, which will spread into every other part of their daily routine.

The Three-a-Day plan means just that: eating three good, fulfilling, nutritious meals, which will help them in many areas. It is a nurturing way to honour the child, his body and state of mind and the practice of thinking ahead to plan their meals is a way of taking good care of their emotional wellbeing. And for snacks in between Three-a-Day, I would recommend some of the Five-a-Day fruit and vegetables.

With these two concepts you can really bring in some good-mood food, some balance, lots of nutrition and some great habits. Wouldn't it be great if you saw the amazing difference in your child just by changing their diet? It's worth a shot.

It's not always easy

It's not always easy to change food routines so here are some ideas to help smooth the way.

1. Become a parent with authority.
Authoritative parenting is the middle ground between a lenient and a strict parent. A lenient parent may allow copious amounts of high-calorie snacks, which are always easily available, and strict parents may strictly forbid such snacks. Parents with authority have a firm but flexible structure for when and how to enjoy a variety of foods as snacks.

Limiting snacks is a middle ground by showing kids how to make decisions about eating wisely. Children need limits and guidance, but the evidence is quite strong that strictly prohibiting foods usually backfires later on when kids have more independence. But, being so liberal with snacks and portions also leads to overeating. Primary school children generally stop eating when they feel full, while adolescents will eat beyond fullness when consistently exposed to large portions. Overeating will expand children's bodies and their stomach capacity as they override their 'I'm full' signals until eating too much becomes a habit.

A good guide is the 80/20 rule. Eating good-mood food 80 per cent of the time while eating snacks and highly processed foods 20 per cent of the time seems to work both nutritionally and for parents.

2. Eat moderately.
Children are better at copying than listening so a family-based approach is wise. Research by Mintel in February 2004 found that more than one in four adults in the UK are trying to lose weight 'most of the time'. The survey estimates that this means that thirteen million people are effectively on a permanent diet. Almost two in five (37 per cent) women were dieting most of the time, compared to around just one in six (18 per cent) of men. The word 'dieting' encompasses binge eating followed by restrictive eating and these habits are likely to be passed on to children. Children do not naturally restrict food and then overeat later unless they learn this behaviour from an adult. Parents can seize the opportunity to become agents of change by a new eating routine. *Superfoods to Boost Your Mood* is a good starting point.

3. Share meals.

Sharing meals has been found to boost the mental health of children. A study published in the *Journal of Epidemiology and Community Health* in January 2002 showed that teenagers from families who eat together appear to have fewer mental health problems, and a third of families of adolescents with mental health problems ate dinner separately compared with just over 17 per cent of the families with healthy youngsters. Researchers suggest sharing meals is a 'unifying ritual', which promotes adolescent mental health.

Not only is it a good time to mull over the day and any worries the children might have but also, when parents are sharing a meal with the children, they are leading by example by eating the right foods, showing good table manners, finishing their plate etc. – all the things we want our children to do.

Children aged nine to fourteen who eat with their parents are likely to have healthier eating habits than those who rarely eat with parents according to a study by Harvard University in July 2005. Family meals were associated with healthy foods: more fruits and vegetables, less processed food and fizzy drinks and more fibre, vitamins and minerals, which will lead to happier children. And one piece of brilliant research shows that eating dinner frequently with your children reduces their risk of substance abuse. A study from the National Center on Addiction and Substance Abuse at Columbia University demonstrated that children from families that almost never eat dinner together are 72 per cent likelier than the average teenager to use illegal drugs, cigarettes and alcohol, while those from families that almost always eat dinner together are 31 per cent less likely than the average teenager to engage in these activities.

My Top Tip:

I introduced this system two years ago when the pressure of
fulfilling everyone's needs, being pressed for time and trying
to force food down my children all came to a head and I had
to find a better way of feeding the family. We all sat down
and planned what everyone wanted to eat then negotiated a
plan for our main meal of the day. It has turned out to be a
brilliant way of getting everyone involved in the family meal.
Because everyone has 'ownership' of the meal plan, it was
easier to get them to agree to it. It goes something like this:

> Monday – Pasta
> Tuesday – Mum's healthy tea
> Wednesday – Chicken roast
> Thursday – Rice dish
> Friday – Fish
> Saturday – Nursery tea
> Sunday – Meat roast

It is simple and effective and I have full control of content
and, so long as I produce meals within these parameters,
it has stopped the complaining that I used to get when I
produced a surprise. The whole family gets excited by what's
on the table that day and anticipates their favourite when
it comes round. I even have the small child eating mackerel
and sprats (very nutritious and very cheap food!) on a Friday.
What is so amazing is that they love the consistency of the
same type of meal every week. I will change the menu about
every three months, but we renegotiate and it's pretty simple
now.

Of course there are days when I can't produce what they
asked for and they get something different but they blend in
because they know what's on offer 80 per cent of the time.
It's a bit like school dinners! They have a rota of food and the

children seem to like the simplicity of the schedule and my philosophy is – if it works, don't fix it!

4. Cultivate a preference for healthier alternatives.
The scientific evidence that fruits and vegetables are critically important to a happier mood is piling up so rapidly that there is a proposal to change the 'Five-a-Day to 'Five-to-Nine-a-Day'.

Tips to achieve this:

❋ If you want the children to eat their vegetables, assume that everyone in the family will do it rather than focus on one child who won't eat their vegetables. For example, instead of . . . 'unless you eat up your vegetables you will be punished with . . .' try fostering a new approach with something like 'Oh, you haven't finished your meal yet, Jamie . . .' and encourage him rather than fight him. If he's used to being let off the hook with vegetables then it will take persistence, but here's a secret...

❋ Don't feed them on high sugar, fat or salt snacks in between meals because they will be full when they get to the table and they can get away with not eating much.

❋ Make fruit and vegetables delicious. Most children I know love a sliced carrot dipped in something like houmous (some kids will eat almost any new food as long as they can dip it), or a small plate of sliced cucumber, or a chopped up apple. Make it look delectable and, if it's a new food, serve it to children when you know there is at least one who's going to say 'Yummy!' and tuck in because this makes it all the more appealing.

❋ Instead of repeatedly buying and serving the same vegetables and fruits, try buying and tasting one new fruit or vegetable every week. Have a weekly ceremony to taste the new produce item and make it into the 'new fruit/vegetable' game: take a bite, then discuss the colour, texture and where the item comes from.

❋ Don't assume a child doesn't like a fruit or vegetable because he or she refused to eat it the first couple of times it was offered. Try waiting a few months and then reintroduce it in a slightly different way.

Recipes for some Good Mood Food

Here are some ideas for great food with mood-boosting qualities. All the recipes are for a family of two adults and two children.

Stuffed baked potato with broccoli on the side

An old favourite with kids
4 large potatoes
50g butter
100g grated cheese
800g broccoli

Method
1. Simply place the potatoes in a hot oven, 200°C/400°F/ Gas Mark 6, for 1¼ hours. If you are short of time you can place them in a microwave oven for 4–5 minutes, depending on the power, until their skins are soft to touch and then place them in the oven for 30 minutes.
2. Once they are cooked, cut each potato in half, scoop out the flesh into a bowl, add the butter and cheese and mix thoroughly. Place the filling back into the potato skins and place back in the oven for 15 minutes.
3. Meanwhile, get the broccoli into a steamer or a pan of simmering water, cover and leave until cooked which will be approximately 10 minutes. Serve together.

Eggy fried rice
A great way to get kids into rice

4 portions cooked rice (using approximately 200g uncooked rice)
85g carrots, diced
1 tbsp olive oil
2 eggs
25g butter
1 bunch spring onions, finely sliced
1 tbsp light soy sauce
85g frozen peas

Method

1. Cook the diced carrots in a pan of simmering water and, just before they are soft, tip in the frozen peas. Once the peas are cooked, drain the vegetables and set aside.
2. Heat the oil in a small frying pan (about 20cm) and lightly beat the eggs in a separate bowl. Pour the eggs into the pan to coat the base, and cook until almost set as a thin omelette – this should take about 2–3 minutes. Flip the omelette over and cook for a few seconds more, then slide it out of the pan and roll it up into a sausage shape. Keep warm.
3. Melt the butter in a wok or large frying pan and sauté the spring onions for 1 minute. Fluff up the rice mixture with a fork (there should be no cooking liquid left). Tip the rice into the wok with the light soy sauce, carrots and peas, then stir fry for 2 minutes. Divide half the rice into four bowls, cut the omelette crossways into strips and scatter over the top. (Keep the remaining rice in a cool place for later.) Serve on its own as a snack or with a piece of chicken or some steamed vegetables.

Forest fruit smoothie
Berries contain an impressive amount of antioxidants, which boost the mood, and this smoothie contains 1–2 portions of fruit per child

Handful of forest fruit, which you buy for the freezer and will last for several smoothies
2 chopped apples
2 chopped bananas or any other combination of fruit you want to try
A splash of fruit juice

Method
1. Simply blend all the ingredients in a blender or smoothie maker until they are smooth. A great 'pick me up' for when the children get back from school.

Fish with the simplest and best tomato sauce
No need to mess with this recipe; it really is as simple as it looks

Serves 4
2 × 400g/14oz tins chopped tomatoes
6 tbsp/100ml olive oil
Handful basil leaves
4 portions of fish of your choice

Method
1. Place the tomatoes into a pan and simmer for 15 minutes or until thick and glossy. Add the olive oil and heat for another 5 minutes. Meanwhile, chop the basil leaves finely and add to the tomato mixture just before taking it off the heat. Pour the sauce over some fresh fish and oven bake. To serve, simply steam some green vegetables and rice.

Home-made pizza
Keep it simple

Make up a tomato sauce as above and pour over a pizza base. Add all your favourite ingredients including sliced onions, peppers and mushrooms for a really healthy pizza. Serve with a salad or sweet corn.

Pasta and pesto (with broccoli)
Children love the pesto

500g dried pasta
500g broccoli
1 tub (150g) pesto
Grated cheese

1. Steam the broccoli until tender. Meanwhile, put a bag of dried pasta (penne is good) into a pan of simmering water and cook according to instructions.
2. Once they are both cooked, drain the broccoli and pasta. Mash the broccoli up into the pasta and pour the tub of pesto into the pasta and broccoli. Serve immediately, with a sprinkling of cheese.

Pan-Grilled Chicken Breast
Preparation time is a minimum. While the chicken is cooking you can get the vegetables on and the table laid

1 chicken breast per person or two children
Olive oil or clarified butter

Method
1. Heat an iron griddle pan over a medium-high heat. Brush each breast with olive oil. Place the chicken on the hot

pan and cook for 3–4 minutes until golden, then change the position and cook for a further 3–4 minutes, so you get criss-cross markings. Repeat on the other side – the chicken should take 15–20 minutes in total to cook. If the breasts are large, you can transfer the pan to a preheated oven (180°C/gas 4) for 8–15 minutes to finish cooking.

2. Once the chicken breasts are cooked, serve with mashed sweet potato or swede and some green beans. Add a knob of butter to the vegetables to make them go down easily.

Ratatouille with fried shallots

A dish for when you have a bit more time. The B3 from the courgettes will help fatigue and depression

Ratatouille:
1 tbsp olive oil
2 chopped red onions
8 courgettes, chopped
250ml/½ pint red wine
2 cloves crushed garlic
450g/14oz can chopped tomatoes
Small can tomato purée
Bunch chopped basil

Fried shallots:
6 shallots, thinly sliced
25g/1oz wholewheat flour
6 tbsp sunflower oil

To serve:
Steamed brown rice

Method

1. Heat the oil in a frying pan, over a moderate heat, then add the red onions. Sauté for 2–3 minutes. Add the courgettes and sauté for a further 2–3 minutes. Add the red wine, crushed garlic, tinned tomatoes and the tomato purée; stir well and allow to reduce for 3–4 minutes. Add the chopped basil and keep warm.

2. Meanwhile, dust the sliced shallots with the flour. Heat the sunflower oil in a pan and fry the shallots for 2 minutes or until they are golden brown. Place the shallots top of the ratatouille dish and serve with steamed brown rice.

Roast tomato risotto

A stunning risotto, which is worth the wait

Serves 4

500g/1lb tomatoes
6 tbsp/90ml olive oil
1 small butternut squash
1 onion, finely chopped
320g/12oz good risotto rice
300ml/10fl oz stock
300mls/10fl oz white wine
Bunch chopped parsley
Pinch dried sage
3 crushed garlic cloves
50g/2oz pecorino Romano cheese, grated

Method

1. Place the tomatoes on a baking tray and drizzle them with half the olive oil. Place them into a preheated oven, 200C/400F/Gas Mark 6. Roast for 30 minutes until the tomatoes are well cooked, soft and squishy.

2. Peel the squash and chop the flesh into small pieces. Place the other half of the olive oil in a large heavy saucepan and gently fry the squash and chopped onions until they are soft.

3. Add the tomatoes and mix then stir in the rice and turn the whole mixture for 2 minutes. Add enough stock to just cover the rice. As the rice absorbs the stock, about 5 minutes, add some more stock to cover the rice and then continue with the white wine until the entire liquid is absorbed.

4. Now, add the herbs, garlic and cheese and mix on a low heat for 2 minutes. Serve immediately – this dish needs no accompaniment!

The family roast with brazil nut stuffing

The Brazil nuts will boost your child's selenium intake – a must for giving them a boost

Serves 4
1 chicken or small turkey weighing about 1.3kg
1 tbsp olive oil
Freshly ground pepper
2 tbsp sunflower oil
Seasonal vegetables
2 potatoes per person, partly boiled
1 tbsp flour and 500ml stock for gravy
Brazil Nut Stuffing:
3 tbsp olive oil
1 large onion, chopped
2 garlic cloves, chopped
400g/12oz chopped Brazil nuts
50g/2oz sunflower seeds, toasted
Bunch chopped sage
100g/4oz fresh coarse whole-wheat breadcrumbs
2 eggs, lightly beaten

Method

1. Firstly make the stuffing. Heat the oil in a large frying pan over a medium heat. Add the onion and cook gently for 3–5 minutes. Add the garlic and cook for 3 minutes. Take off the heat. Add the Brazil nuts, sunflower seeds, breadcrumbs and eggs. Mix well and place into a greased baking dish.

2. Preheat the oven to 200°C/400°F/Gas Mark 6. Place the chicken/turkey in a roasting tin and drizzle with 1 tbsp olive oil. Grind the black pepper over the top. Place into the preheated oven. After 30 minutes, place the partly boiled potatoes on another tin and drizzle with the sunflower oil. Place them in the top of the oven. The chicken/turkey should be ready in one hour.

3. Place the stuffing into the oven 30 minutes before the chicken/turkey is ready. Prepare your vegetables and put them on to cook 15 minutes before you are due to serve. Take out the chicken/turkey and place the bird on a tray for carving.

4. Make your gravy: drain off the excess fat from the roasting tin in which the bird was cooked, add the flour and stock to the pan and whisk until thick. Serve immediately.

Cook's tip: Gravy powder now comes in a low-salt version. This is a quick and easy alternative for making gravy.

Exercise

Children who get regular exercise are happier than children who watch TV or play computer games according to research published by the BBC in February 2006. Children who exercise once a week or less were four times more likely to say they were unhappy, and five times more likely to have few or no friends. Children who got *no* exercise were found to be more likely to argue with their parents and have a stressful home life. Exercise can help people lift depression.

A study, published in the *British Journal of Sports Medicine* in October 2006, stated that a simple exercise programme can substantially improve depression scores in patients with moderate to severe major depression, despite prior failures with medication.[28]

Not only does exercise help with depression but increasingly researchers are finding that brain activity and brain development are enhanced by physical exercise. It now appears that exercise can help kids learn at school and this will add to a child's self-esteem and generally lift their spirits.

The biggest influence on children's exercise is parents. The more parents exercise, the more children exercise. When physical activity is a family affair, your child is less likely to perceive it as a chore, but instead it is something they look forward to each day.

You can sit down and talk about what sports each family member enjoys and then come up with a plan of activities that fit in your schedule. Some ideas include swimming, walking somewhere that's fun like a forest or beach, biking to a park, bowling, dancing, tennis, squash or Rollerblading.

Playing outdoor games together is another way to keep your family physically active. Instead of sitting down to

---

28 'A randomised, controlled study on the effects of a short-term endurance training programme in patients with major depression', Dr F. Dimeo, of the Benjamin Franklin Medical Centre, in Berlin, Germany

watch television after dinner, go into the garden and play a ball game. Not only will playing together nurture a family connection, it will also help to build strong bones and muscles and increase cardiovascular endurance. All of these activities will help a child's self-esteem and lift depression.

SETTING BOUNDARIES

Children in a family are like flowers in a bouquet: there's always one determined to face in an opposite direction from the way the arranger desires.

Marcelene Cox, writer

Unconditional love is at one end of the parenting spectrum and setting boundaries is at the other. Setting boundaries with love is how it works best for a depressed child. A lack of consistent boundaries can be one of the main reasons that children become depressed. There aren't enough support systems for kids, and the rules for what is acceptable behaviour have been blown away. Kids function best with boundaries and there aren't many today. A lack of boundaries results in a lack of stability and this is a key factor for enabling children to feel unsafe, discontented and 'out of sorts'.

Children who have had no boundaries don't develop their own sense of self-control and will carry on behaving like toddlers who get away with anything even at eighteen years old. A boundary-*less* childhood can lead the child into a damaging adulthood as they can end up being very unhappy and lonely. In setting boundaries we are teaching children to set their own limits and teaching them to trust themselves, and how far they can push the limits.

We seem to be protecting our children more and more from challenges and the vital lessons of disappointment.

We seem to be fearful that our children will not be able to rise up to even the most routine tasks of tidying their room, turning up somewhere on time and being responsible for their own homework. It is crucial that they learn that there are self-fulfilling rewards and consequences that go with self-responsibility. But it's happening in our whole society and we seem to have lost our direction when it comes to setting boundaries. Rather like we have come to accept that processed food is normal food we are losing sight of the basic ingredients that we need to get wholesome results and the results we are getting are 'processed' kids.

The headline Lost Childhoods was published in the *Daily Telegraph* in September 2006 following a letter that had been sent to the paper, signed by a group of 110 influential experts. It said that junk food, computer games, relentless marketing and competitive schooling are making British children depressed. 'Modern life leads to more depression among young children,' it said, claiming that interaction with adults, and time to be children have given way to junk food, sedentary, screen-based entertainment, and a test-driven curriculum and that children today act and dress like mini-adults and are exposed to 'material that would have been considered unsuitable for them even in the very recent past'. Society, they argue, is preoccupied with protecting children from physical harm but has lost sight of their emotional and social needs, leading to an escalation in childhood depression, substance abuse, violence and self-harm.

However, the majority of these children are not raised by the state, they are raised by parents. And these statements portray an absolvent of any influence that parents have. But these statements are wrong. When the child comes home from school, the parents have the choice to feed them good food, turn the television off, turn the computer off and take them out for some exercise. Why is this so hard to do?

Perhaps because the boundaries have been wobbly and the kids have done what kids do best – pleaded, cried for, begged for and yelled for what they want and, for an easy life, we have given in. There is no greater power than 'pester power' but it can be halted and the boundaries can be redrawn.

Let's get one thing straight, children love boundaries – they love them! They love to feel safe by having the lines of fairness drawn around them, keeping them folded into their life. Having boundaries laid down is like having someone firmly tuck the blanket around you when you're lying in bed and then instructing you not to get out until the morning. Yes it's restrictive but it's safe. As long as the boundary being set is fair then the child knows it's right. Boundaries are the second most important thing you can give a child after unconditional love.

It is extremely helpful to a depressed child to know what the boundaries are. It's also very helpful for children to be able to rely on the boundaries staying consistent. If the boundaries are fair and consistent, this gives the child a sense of security that it can learn to rely on. While relying on the boundaries staying the same, the child can gain a sense of calm. The child can come to rely on the everyday routine as rock solid and adjust himself accordingly.

However, they may not show they like the boundaries you've set and create mayhem when you tell them they can't have any more television after a certain time. That's not to say the boundaries are not right; it is to say that they may not like them; however, the boundaries are staying!

When setting and sticking to boundaries it can seem extremely punishing to us, the parents, as we say to ourselves, 'I'm sure I'm doing the right thing' yet feeling that we are somehow *abusing* the child and the child is deliberately trying to get back at the parents by rebuking them to a point of no return. It is easy to change the boundaries with an 'OK just this once…' approach and allow the child to score a point over us because we want an easy life.

Here's a concept that is a great way of keeping objective while setting the boundaries; the 'mini-drunk'. Remind yourself of it when you have just set the new rule and your child is having a massive tantrum or flailing himself around the room in complete rebellion of your authority. It may keep you sane.

The mini-drunk

A child is a curly dimpled lunatic.

Ralph Waldo Emerson, philosopher

There is one principle about children that is universal – children are 'mini-drunks' and if you can grasp this whole concept you will find setting the boundaries much easier. It will help to lay down the boundaries with a sense of impartiality and detachment while dealing with the most difficult behaviour. All children are mini-drunks and to what extent they're drunk depends on their age.

Newborn
When they are first born they are paralytic. They can't do anything for themselves, not even lift up their head. They scream and wail, throw up, cannot eat solids and it's all you can do to stop them killing themselves by rolling off a surface or choking to death. There is no difference in the behaviour of a baby and a fully inebriated adult.

Toddlers
As they grow into toddlers, they wobble and fall over, have no rhyme nor reason, scream at the merest hint of something they don't like and fight you all the way with eating, bathing, dressing etc.

3–6 years

As children grow the drunkenness gradually wears off. They are no longer paralytic but they are drunk enough to 'lose it' when they don't get their own way; watch a four-year-old throw a tantrum and compare it to the erraticism of someone who is drunk and creates havoc after being told 'no'. You have to have a little respect for their outbursts; at least they are direct!

7–13 years

Once they reach seven the effects are lessened, where they throw the occasional outburst but are becoming more coherent and more able to speak like an adult. As they grow into adolescents they are like a drunk who's almost sober because they can reason with you but they are limited by their lack of common sense.

14–20 years

By the time they reach adolescence, they are well and truly 'hung over' and behave as though they have a massive headache, grunt when spoken to and seem a little unfocused. Their confused and fuzzy brain can sometimes be a little worrying! Anyone who knows a teenager will understand this. Even talking to a teenager is reminiscent of someone suffering the morning after the night before.

21+ years

However, by 21 they have sobered up and have become quite human; by 25 they are well and truly recovered.

While you're dealing with a child whose behaviour seems 'way over the top', just look at them as though they are drunk. Drunks know no better and, in the same way, children know no better. By having a little detachment it is possible to giggle to yourself while your child writhes around the floor or stomps off in a huff having been refused something he wants.

But it's not personal

If you can grasp the 'it's not personal' concept you will recognise that the child's unwillingness to do what you say and his inability to stay rational when you give a command is not personal to you. By understanding that the child would behave with *anyone in this way who was their parent* it might help you to stay composed, which will pay dividends towards the relationship you have with your child.

As you grasp the idea that your child's reaction to you is not about you, you will be able to uphold a sense of detachment. This detachment is the best stance to take when you set any limits/rules/boundaries because it will protect you from any possible backlash you may receive and be influenced by. The best schoolteachers can teach parents so much about parenting as they are able to practise the art of detachment in a firm but fair way, which leaves everyone with a win/win outcome. If you have the opportunity to spend an hour with your child's favourite teacher when they are around children it will be worth a month of parenting classes. (As a school governor I know how short staffed schools are and volunteering as a classroom assistant may be very welcome.)

They are only doing their job

Once you have established the concepts of the 'mini-drunk' and 'it's not personal to you', you can grasp the fact that they are 'only doing their job'. It's the children's job to push as hard on their own limits as they possibly can. It's their job to fight the rules and make a demand that their needs be met. It's part of their own growth to challenge, question and tackle what they are presented with. It's part of the natural human development for all children to do this – it's their job!

And we are only doing ours.

As the adult, it's our job to keep the limits tight and to keep the children confined to the rules until they have relaxed and learned the boundaries. Setting a boundary is just like breaking in a young horse. Before some new education has taken place, a young horse will throw himself around and rear up on his hind legs when you attempt to place a saddle on his back for the first time. This is no different to the child throwing himself on the ground and bawling like a demented hyena when you have told him he cannot go out to play until his toys are put away. You get out of the young horse's stable and watch over the stable door until he has calmed down. Humour is a great antidote for such outbursts. Whenever possible, help children to see the humour in a difficult situation. Responding to an angry outburst in a calm way with a gentle smile will often help diffuse the child's fury. Crack a one-liner, if not to him then to yourself. My husband often says something like 'Bit of an epic today!' or 'I'll have to consult my lawyer on this!' while our son is hanging on to the door handle for all he's worth, refusing to go upstairs for his bath. Learning to laugh or joke about the tantrum helps children put things in perspective. Next time the saddle goes on there will be less disruption and after a few sessions of consistent training, the child (and the horse) will be completely at ease about the new rule.

The key to a successful relationship in the battle of a child's determination is … Well, who has the answer? No one! Everyone's experience is different and everyone's outcome is different. But the concept is the same everywhere and it keeps the rules of engagement clear and clean. If depression is affected by wavering boundaries, resetting them is a good place to get started.

How to set boundaries

For everything there is a season,
And a time for every matter under heaven:
A time to be born, and a time to die;
A time to plant, and a time to pluck up what is planted;
A time to kill, and a time to heal;
A time to break down, and a time to build up.

Ecclesiastes 3

Setting boundaries with a sense of detachment will:

✳ help your child feel better about themselves
✳ get some order within the family system
✳ help you feel better about you
✳ restore some respect between you and your child

Here are five suggestions to follow when setting new boundaries:

1. One at a time

Set one boundary at a time. If you allow the child to settle into a new routine and get used to the new rule, you will find the second boundary you put in place will become easier and the third easier still. Start by identifying one area which is rocky. Ascertain what new rule needs to be inaugurated without delay. If you aren't sure what the new rule should be, ask a teacher or another parent with whom you have respect. For example, what time should a thirteen-year-old go to bed? Ensure you feel happy with the new rule and that you can confidently parent your child with it. Also, make sure it is within your own realm of understanding and influence; for example, some parents may allow their kids to stay up until 10 p.m. but you don't feel that's good for your family so attune what others say to your own belief system because if you feel good about the new rule your child will come to feel good about it.

2. Give warning

Children like to know what's going to happen in advance so they can get prepared. If you can give an appropriate warning of a new rule then you are more likely to get a better response. For example, 'From Monday night your bedtime is going to be 9 p.m.' We are no different; if something is going to happen that involves change for us we like to be informed so we can organise ourselves.

3. Take action

Once you have prepared the child for the change, implement the boundary as and when you said you would. Stay close to the plan you gave the child so they are reassured by your firmness.

4. Don't waver

Having said that, no one said it would be easy! You will come up against some pretty strong objections, such as the child throwing a massive wobbly and hurling himself across the supermarket floor, like a hockey puck on ice, after you have just explained to him that the new rule is now in place and 'No' he cannot have any crisps today.

The child, if he has any sense (and they are generally much more sensible than we give them credit for) will try to talk you out of the new rule by wailing that no other friends have to go through this tortuous new statute that they have to go through and isn't it just so unfair that he is the only one that this has ever happened to ... DON'T WAVER. If the child sees a flicker of hesitancy he will have you over a barrel before you know what's hit you. You must also be prepared in the full knowledge that this new rule is to help your child feel better about himself, which will go a million miles towards addressing their depression.

5. Allow a long enough lead time
Allow plenty of time for the new rule to settle down. A long lead time will help establish the boundary and then you are ready to put the next one in place. You may want to keep a note in your diary about what you want to change – week by week.

Three things to bear in mind when setting new boundaries:

1. Establish the new boundaries to fulfil your estranged needs as well as setting the pace for a new routine at home. It is very, very important to the child that his parent is OK. This is explained more fully in Chapter 4 'The Family Affair', but suffice to say that the child needs a happy parent in order to be able to resolve their own difficulties so it's vital to make sure you get the boundaries right for you. For example, if a child is playing up at bedtime, every night, and insists on staying up later than you would like and not giving you the time you need to relax then you will not get through the evening without feeling stressed. Inevitably, the child loses out because he does not get the best possible care from you. This will diminish his self-worth because all children, no matter who they are, take on board that they are somehow responsible for the parent's unhappiness.
2. If the child is getting away with murder it is because the parent is allowing him to get away with murder.
3. Don't tell your child in advance of the whole plan unless you wish to unleash the devil; keep to one change at a time.

As weird as it may sound, always remember one thing: your child is not the parent, you are. How easy it is to feel that our child is so powerful they dictate to us. And how easy it is for us to lose our own supremacy! Just knowing that it happens is enough to get us back on track with our kids!

☎ BUILDING THE TEAM

It takes a village to raise a child.

Kenyan proverb

Building a team of people around your child can be extremely satisfying and helpful to both you and your child. You can find people who are willing to support him through his recovery from depression and that will encourage his own sense of worth as well as maintain your determination to champion him.

Finding a therapist

If you feel that you need some specialist help then finding a therapist for your child could be a good start. A therapist should have experience of childhood depression and qualifications to back this up. Your GP should be able to help you find a therapist and is a good source. But if they can't then you may have to find one privately. If this is the case there are several options.

Before you start I would recommend that you do lots of research and ask lots of questions before you send your child to anyone. Recommendations from other parents, school, children's services etc. are the best way to find a good therapist. Please make sure you do your homework because there are lots of charlatans working as therapists. But there are also some highly skilled people who will understand child development and be able to quickly get to the heart of the child's depression and help him recover. You will probably be asked to step in as part of his therapy.

For younger children a good starting point is play therapy. Play therapy helps children understand muddled feelings and upsetting events that they haven't had the chance to sort out properly. Rather than having to explain what is troubling them, as adult therapy usually requires, children use play to communicate at their own level and at their own pace, without feeling interrogated or threatened. For adolescents, there are therapists who are trained in helping this age group and for children of both ages; sources for these counsellors can be found in the back of the book.

School

Schools can be a fantastic resource for your child's team. The best way to start is to have a meeting with your child's teacher and explain what's happening at home and with your child. Teachers are so much better able to manage depressive symptoms if they have all the information. One suggestion is to write a 'paper' on your child's little ways, which will help your child but also help the teacher. It can list all of the things he will or won't eat, how he is responding at the moment, advice on the right question to ask to get the best from him and where his vulnerabilities lie etc. without it turning into a thesis. You could send in a short update every few weeks to let the teacher know how well his recovery is going. The response you receive from the teacher may surprise you; although they seemed so pressed for time, information about a child which will help their job can enhance a teacher's work.

College

Teenagers really don't like parents getting involved in their affairs once they reach fourteen or fifteen. Once they are sixteen it's just embarrassing! In spite of their awareness of the world, they are not self-aware and still need lots of help. Colleges have plenty to offer with great facilities and counsellors, special needs and dyslexia teams. Take advantage of them and go and see them. They are funded to help our teenagers. One call can really bring the attention of the specialist to the teenager and the extra interest in the teenager can make all the difference to their confidence and self-esteem. Not only will they keep a special eye on their 'client', but they can also feed back the teenager's progress and this can help you to help your teenager achieve his best potential.

Sports

Sport is a great advocate for depressed children. Not only does exercise boost the mood and lift depression, but being supported by an enthusiastic coach can really help a child whose self-worth is low. The key to getting a child started in a sport is to get involved too. Research shows that the more a parent shows interest and *support* for a child's sport, the more positive the child feels about the sport and the better he feels about himself.[29] Conversely, the more *pressure* a parent shows, the less the child enjoys the sport and he feels more negative about the sport.

Getting the child started is easier if the parent is involved and once the parent is involved they can assess the teachers and coaches who would be suitable as a mentor for the child. As the child gains confidence, they may find they want to have the parents around less. Conversely, it might be a great way for the child and parent to have some value time together by becoming really good at a sport that can

29 S. S. Leff and R. H. Hoyle, 'Young athletes' perceptions of parental support and pressure', *Journal of Youth and Adolescence*, 24 (1995), 187–203

accommodate all ages. Rock climbing is a good example of this. Even young children can take part and will soon overtake the parent in aptitude and ability. Once this has happened it's time for the parent to step aside and let the coach take over.

Family and extended family

Families seem very separated these days and it's not unusual for a family to be living some distance from their extended family. The modern family is changing and it is becoming accepted practice to embrace people who are not family members and make them a part of the family circle. This is especially true with babysitters, nannies, child minders and teachers; when the children have grown up the people who have helped care for the child may become a part of the family's life and can be enveloped in familiarity and love by being included in parties, weddings, Christmas celebrations etc.

Other such people are priests or vicars, close family friends, godparents, past teachers, people who share a passion for sport or other leisure pursuits. And now, as the new 'extended' family is becoming the norm, parents of step-children and half brothers and sisters are becoming familial.

People love to be able to help, and to mobilise the affection that these people have for your depressed child can take an adult from being interested in their wellbeing to being passionate about their recovery. It's amazing how people can rise to the occasion if they are asked and how much compassion they have. There's a lot more good in people than we realise and sometimes all it takes is to ask for help. People often hold back because they think their help is not wanted.

The influence of an adult who is not a parent can be very beneficial. Children need approval from adults who are not their parents. This strengthens their sense of self and that will help a child recover from depression. You can play an active role in finding role models for your child. One question to ask yourself is, is this the kind of person I want my child to be like? This will give you a good indication of whether or not this person might be good for your child. This is especially important if you are a single-parent family. Be bold, be brave and be concerned. Your efforts could make every difference to your child.

Chapter 4
A Family Affair

👋 THE IMPORTANCE OF FAMILY

To a child, his family is everything: his home, his heart, his fountain of love, his guide, his refuge, his cloud on which to lie when he needs the gentleness of a familiar lullaby. The family is the social structure that holds a child safely until the time comes for him to move out into the world of expectation and hope. He will have learned how to nourish himself, how to gain a balance between dependence and autonomy, learn the moral code for a valued life and have the tools to maximise his potential. Like a strong shoot that has been separated from the mother plant, a child leaves the family soil and will grow his own set of roots, which will feed and strengthen him for the rest of his life. How this young shoot takes root is very dependent on the health of the family plant.

As a child faces the relentless prospects of being confronted with adverse circumstances outside the home, the best therapy he can hope for is that the family offers him a safe place in which to retreat and reform his experiences of bullying, peer pressure, exposure to emotional abuse or drugs. He can learn from his experiences through the family's guidance and support and venture out the following day full of confidence in his ability to protect himself. He will be able to be a part of a supportive peer group, which allows him to be himself, learning to measure himself as he goes and recognising people and situations that may compromise his safety. He will be able to set his own limits and say 'no' to those circumstances that are not beneficial to him. This is what helps a child develop his own sense of freedom and personal potential. And this is what will make a child happy. The supportive family is like a pinball machine where the child can go bounce around the interior of the pinball's engine, safely, without recrimination or judgement and with navigation by the family, and finally come out the other end to enjoy another day.

The type of family that is able to support the child in this way is full of love, challenged but excited, willing to make changes in the light of new experience, able to be open about what is troubling the family as a whole. Adults gain as much fulfilment as the children because they will be open to the honesty and refreshing approach that the children bring to the table. Of course the parents will be more or less content in their own life but they will not see themselves as perfect and they would be willing to receive open feedback about their ideas or behaviours and take what they want, leaving behind the comments that don't interest them. They will generally feel safe in their own skin and know how do deal with the knocks of life, thereby having the ability to teach their children these life skills.

A trailblazer in the field of family therapy, Christian Midelfort published the findings of his research on the relationships between his depressed clients and their families. He concluded his study with the words 'This study substantiates the idea that all emotional illness develops in a family and is present in several members of the family.'[30]

If the family is depressed, then the outcome for the child's emotional health will be different. A depressed family increases the odds of having a depressed child. But I have never met a family who sets out to do this. I have never met an adult who says, 'I chose to treat my child this way in order to make him depressed.' No, it doesn't work that way. It may be that we haven't challenged our own parent's values; it could be that we didn't know how much our own emotional health would impact on our children; it might be that we did know but we just didn't have the power to

---

30 *The Family in Psychotherapy* (New York: McGraw Hill, 1957)

change it. Whatever the reason may be, I have never met a parent who was intentionally trying to inhibit a child's emotional wellbeing.

In acknowledging your child's emotional imbalance, you are on the starting block of recovery for both you and your child. It's the acceptance that counts. Here we examine the shape of a *depressed* family and the shape of a *contented* family.

❀ THE DEPRESSED FAMILY

The depressed family is a family who cannot share their concerns about the world for fear of criticism or judgement. It is a family that is anxious about them but is afraid to expose those anxieties. This family maybe more concerned with the way it is viewed from the outside and less concerned with what happens within it. There will be little communication between the family members and this allows the family to foster a culture of everyone having to keep things to themselves. This family will be nervous of each other, hiding matters that bother them for fear of recrimination or feeling ashamed of something they've done. This translates into 'contaminated shame'.

Contaminated shame
'Contaminated shame' is rife in a depressed family; this is where each person does not feel good about who they are – their very being. It's the engine that drives a depressed family because the 'contaminated shame' needs to be kept hidden. 'Contaminated shame' leaves us feeling that we are worse than anyone else and the fear that someone might find this out drives us to keep the secret out of sight. All our actions are governed by how we can dodge being 'found out' because being 'found out' would be unbearable. Or would it?

Ironically, the very thing that holds us back from exposing our 'contaminated shame' is the very thing that will heal us. Exposure is the key because 'contaminated shame' is like a bacterium that grows in the dark but exposure to light will begin to clear it out. This is personal growth at its very best and this whole subject is tackled, for adults, in my first book *Beat Depression and Reclaim Your Life*.

'Contaminated shame' was placed in us when we were children. We don't develop 'contaminated shame' as adults. Children will simply copy the adults if they have not acquired enough autonomy in their short life. This is why the whole family needs to be addressed to help the depressed child recover.

The exciting thing about looking at the family's issues is that everyone can feel better about himself or herself. What one does affects everyone else. It's like every member of the family emulating a bauble on a mobile, which hangs from the ceiling. If one person moves, or gets off, everyone is affected. In times of change it is often the child who changes fastest because they don't have the historical baggage adults have. To be hanging onto the coat tail of a child recovering from depression can be an exciting ride.

Here are some concepts with which to look at ways in which the depressed family might be trapped.

Parental depression

It is a proven fact: children of depressed parents have much more chance of suffering from depression themselves. Depression isn't catching but a depressed parent just cannot function in the same way as a parent who isn't depressed. My son looks back at the time when I was very depressed and the one thing he remembers is how quiet I was. Quiet? He should have heard it from the inside. I was having a constant dialogue in my head, churning over my problems, feeling lots of emotional pain, feeling bad and hopeless but simply doing enough to keep us alive. But he says that I never used to say anything. I don't remember it that way. I thought I was being bright and breezy whenever I was with him, trying so hard to cover up the fact that I was feeling like I was in the middle of a bottomless black pit. But he saw it differently to me and no matter how hard I tried to hide my depression, it obviously showed.

The best thing a parent can do for a depressed child is to help himself or herself. *Beat Depression And Reclaim Your Life* is a manual that I wrote with myself in mind and it *does what it says on the can*. And the first thing I recommend to any adult who is depressed – surrender!

When you are depressed, trying to fight it is like trying to stem back the flow of water from the incoming tide. You will wear yourself out just trying and you will never succeed. The best piece of guidance I can offer is to finally, conclusively and completely admit your depression to yourself. The relief that comes from giving up the fight to build all those sandbanks and concrete defences to keep the sea from washing you away, is monumental. It's now, and only now, you can do something to help yourself. After *Beat Depression and Reclaim Your Life* was published, I had many, many people tell me that the very act of surrendering was enough to help them towards the road of recovery. It's the acknowledgment to yourself that all is not well but hope is outside the front door. It's the relief of a child who's been in pain with a tummy ache for a long time and his parent has just noticed and will do something to get help.

Making your child your best friend

There's a sharp change in our society that has us believe that our child can be our best friend. Something's gone amiss; the boundaries have been blurred.

I was talking to one mum from my son's school who was telling a group of us how she likes to go on a camping trip every year with her son. She said, 'Oh it's so much fun. Basically I become the child and Linus becomes the adult. He huffs and puffs while I roam around dropping everything and making such a muck up of it. We have tremendous fun; he goes off surfing and I make sure our nest is ready when he gets back. We are best friends and I always put my camping trip with Linus before anything else.' Linus was sixteen when the mum regaled the camping story. But, it's not right and in truth, the mum would be better off dropping Linus and some mates to the campsite for a camping trip and picking them up at the end of the weekend. Whose needs is the 'best friend' relationship fulfilling? It certainly wasn't Linus's because he was standing next to his mother while she explained their trip and he was squirming so much that I squirmed too.

Jonathan, nineteen, says of his parents: 'Ironically my parents are my worst nightmare because they think they are my best friends. My mum, well, she pushed me and pushed me educationally, forced her life on to me, threw me out when I rebelled and refused to be what she wanted.' Jonathan brings up the point that parents are your best friends until the child becomes a teenager and rails against this relationship because it is not giving the child what he needs.

The reason it is so unequal is that if the parent needs to make a firm stand on a disciplinarian issue, the parent will have to forgo the 'best friends' bit and be the parent. But for the child, this will feel like a betrayal, like having any best friend turn against him. Best friends cannot also serve discipline just as a cake mixture won't turn into a loaf of bread once it's gone in the oven; it's black and white. So you are either the 'best friend' or you are the parent. The child may see you as their best friend and that's realistic. But if the child is used as the parent's best friend, this leads to trouble because the child can no longer be free to be childlike, as they have to take on the burden of the parents' problems. This isn't right for the child and could lead to depression. It's a one-way relationship and that's how it should be.

The family secret

In depressed families there is usually a secret that no one talks about. This secret is surrounded by a wall of shame, denial and defence. The secret often becomes a governing principle around which the family adapts to maintain itself and its fragile family structure.

This secret might be: a scandal, an illicit affair, alcoholism, adoption, sexual abuse, drug abuse, being broke and trying to hide it, food bingeing, gambling, unhappy marriage, domestic violence, child or parental depression. Whatever the secret is, it can be that the covering up of the secret becomes more damaging than the secret itself.

An American psychiatrist, Murray Bowen, was a key figure in the development in family therapy. Beginning in the 1950s, he developed a systems theory of the family. While working at the National Institute of Mental Health, Bowen discussed how families deal with a family secret by means of an emotional cut-off.[31]

Emotional cut-off refers to the mechanisms people use to reduce anxiety from their unresolved emotional issues with parents, siblings and other members from the family of origin. To avoid sensitive issues, they either move away from their families or rarely go home; or, if they remain in physical contact with their families, to avoid sensitive issues, they use silence or divert the conversation.

---

31 Michael E. Kerr and Murray Bowen, *Family Evaluation: An Approach Based on Bowen Theory*

This is also a coping strategy that a family will use when they are harbouring a family secret. They simply don't allow themselves to feel anything about the secret because there is just too much anxiety or pain surrounding it. When you cut off some emotions, you cut off all emotions and so the capacity for joy and peace in a family that is harbouring secrets is lost. In order to suppress a secret, the anger and frustration must also be suppressed and this causes depression. The feeling that is experienced is 'contaminated shame'. Secrets make a family become shame based and this is the core of a depressed family.

Families with a secret also experience misplaced loyalties. The strength of the loyalty assists the family to stay glued together and dam up any leaks. This loyalty can be fierce and trying to uncover the family secret may be difficult because of it. I was sharing my feelings, overtly, on a forum for depressed teenagers and it was intimate and honest. Until, that was, I shared my family's past secrets and asked if they had any family secrets. Bearing in mind they were speaking completely anonymously, first came a rush of the most frightening collection of family secrets I've ever heard and then, within an hour, I was banned form the forum FOREVER for DARING TO ASK THAT QUESTION! The family secret can stir up some powerful allegiances but in whose interests are those allegiances? Can it be good for the depressed teenager to be loyal to the mother who sexually abuses him? No, but if he sees her as his only form of survival then he will.

An extreme example, but it only serves to illustrate the strength of misplaced loyalties. On a less severe scale, our social structure positively promotes misplaced family loyalties. I know many people, when asked how their parents are, who would answer 'Fine' with no other adjective. Yet, it's common knowledge that their parents or families are very depressed, shame-based families who are desperately unhappy, whose sixty-year-old mother is still drinking heavily, whose father will have no contact with them yet they choose to ignore their own feelings of loss. But if people were to confront their own denial and state, when asked how they are, 'My brother's gone missing because his drug addiction has led him to sever contact with me', the listener may turn away because that was just too much information.

There is a book I would recommend you to read if you wish to take a good look at family secrets. It is called *Family Secrets* by John Bradshaw (a well-known American writer of family issues) and it will give you grounding on where to start. He recommends not marching into the arena with all good intentions to make a clean sweep but to use caution, especially those who have experienced heavy abuse, and to take things at a very easy pace, to be gentle with yourself and not to get extreme in the recovery process.

For the purpose of *this* book, by acknowledging there is a family secret, you are paving the way for change and healing and taking the focus off the depressed child who may only be trying to hold onto the family secret and sinking into a mire of depression as a result. By examining the secret and talking about it, the shame will begin to lift. This may be easier than it sounds but talking to someone in confidence, outside the family, can be a good starting point. You will feel liberated from the moment you let the secret slip out of your mouth. To avoid feeling ashamed, make sure you talk to someone who hears this type of secret all the time. For instance, if you want to talk about drug abuse in the family, call a drug abuse line that takes calls like this everyday and will not be phased by your story.

Once the ball has started rolling and the secret is out in the open, everyone will lighten up. It will feel scary because it feels like breaking the family rule 'Don't talk about it'. But that rule needs to be broken, like the dam needs to split, and the built-up pressure will create a gush of water which will sweep away so many other bottled-up concerns.

The roles of the child

Children who live in depressed families usually adopt a specific role within the family. This role helps the child fit into the family system by hiding their true selves and playing a part by placating others and helps them better survive the family depression.

The hero

The heroes tend to be firstborn. They are high achievers, responsible and perfectionist. Becoming academically successful or excelling at sports helps them to feel in control and helps to make their families look good. Although they take responsibility for their family's problems, they are, at the same time, people-pleasers who seek others' approval. Being a hero masks their feelings of loneliness, loss, anger and resentment at not being listened to, not being heard and having to be too grown up too soon.

The family view of the child is *'Ahh, look at Thomas, he's just such a good, hard-working boy; why can't the others be like him? He makes my life so easy, does what he's told and just gets on with it.'* Teachers generally view a hero child as the model pupil but this success traps the hero child in a vicious cycle of trying to be the best, hiding feelings of loneliness and not ever feeling good enough, feeling angry about the pressure but not able to express it, feeling depressed as a result and then working harder to cover it up.

The problem

The 'problem' child is chaotic, expressing his grief, anger and unhappiness by acting out the feelings instead of expressing

them and becoming the bad boy or girl of the family. The
problem child appears to be the big challenge in the family
and this can deflect attention from the other family problems
because everyone can focus on his outrageous behaviour.

It's a paradox because when the problem child acts out
and shocks the family, the repercussions for that child can
be miserable and he is continually blamed for all the family's
problems. This cycle of behaviour and negative feedback can
cause a deep depression because the very core of a child's self-
worth is at stake. It is so difficult for the parents of a problem
child to know what to do because although the child wants
to be accepted as a whole person – and that comes with a
lot of pain and anger – the parents also have to set tight
boundaries on the behaviour to ensure he doesn't become
out of control.

The problem child may also become the scapegoat outside
the home and may indulge in a vicious circle of acting out
problem behaviour then being made a scapegoat, as he gets
blamed for everything.

The family view of the child is *'Oh look at Thomas. How
are we ever going to be happy while he's such a problem?'*

The mascot

Mascot children cope by hiding their inner feelings of pain,
frustration, anger and hurt by becoming jokers or by acting
as if they are happy. As they are celebrated for their humour,
wit and cynicism, the mascot's charmingly buffoonish
behaviour deflects attention away from the family and on
to the mascot. They are the cheerleader of the family and
their whole sense of identity hides the ugliness of the family.
But, there is a lot of insecurity and fear in this child because
what happens if no one thinks they are funny? Who are they
then? When things get tense in the family, that's their cue
to act funny. Often the mascot is the class clown in school;

the other children laugh but the teachers don't. Yet at home the family positively values the mascot, *'What would we do without Thomas? He keeps us all going!'* They encourage the same behaviour that the mascot gets punished for at school.

The lost child

Lost children cope by withdrawing or isolating themselves from their families, denying their hurt and trying to convince themselves that their problems don't exist, to the point where they try not to exist by becoming invisible. The lost child may also become the invisible child in the corner or at the back of the room. This child identifies with the other family members pain and tries to help them but because they can't (because they are children not adults) they usually remove themselves from the situation and become hidden. Because their coping strategy involves removing themselves from situations they can't handle, lost children are generally perceived as shy, sensitive loners. This detachment can help the lost child to gain control and protect himself but it does cost him by losing closeness with other members of the family and friends. This child provides relief for a family – *'At least someone in our family doesn't cause us any problems.'*

Interestingly, if we ourselves had taken up one of these roles as a child, we may still be playing this role in our adult world:

As *the hero* we may end up becoming very successful in our careers but not necessarily fulfilled. We may seek to bury ourselves in work rather than face our feelings of inadequacy and failure.

As *the problem* we may well get ourselves into plenty of trouble, legally and otherwise. We are angry with the world and, once we left home, we found a way of expressing it which may not be to our best interest. We may have struggled with relationships and feel very lonely but not be able to see why.

As *the mascot* we feel compelled to be in the centre stage and consider it our duty to entertain our friends and come across as the life and soul of the party.

As *the lost child,* we don't like to be seen and get panicky about having to do anything that might expose us.

What usually happens is that we take on a main role but can slip into other roles from time to time. My role was generally the 'problem' child but there were times when I became the 'mascot' and found a niche in entertaining everyone and feeling some sense of belonging by doing this. In my early adult life I naturally shifted into these roles when I was particularly stressed or depressed and I wanted to keep other people at a distance. Now, however, if I feel myself slipping into these roles I know that I need to be more honest with myself, and those close to me, about how I'm feeling and what it is I'm trying to avoid.

It is worth taking a look at whether or not we are still role-playing because if we are, we are teaching our children to do the same. By challenging these roles we allow ourselves to be closer to our true selves. By challenging the idea that we have to be in a certain role to please others, we are teaching our children that it's OK to be themselves.

Parental anger

For so long we have been hearing: 'Angry? Let it out', 'Don't hold it in it will harm you' 'Express your feelings' etc. So, when does parental anger become harmful?

Expressing, in a measured voice, anger about something that has affected us is one thing but using anger as a way of self-stimulating feelings of power or to control others' behaviour, especially children, is another. Chronic anger in a parent is belittling, disrespectful, cruel and frightening. I've heard it said '*If you experience a feeling for more than fifteen minutes, it's historic*'; in other words, it's not to do with the present moment, it's unresolved anger from the past.

Having been brought up in an 'angry' house, I know what it feels like to be around that air of tension that only leaves sporadically and usually because something big has happened like the first day of a holiday or winning some money. That didn't happen very often so for the rest of the time I was left with a sense of foreboding and apprehension, trying to predict the mood of the adults in order to avoid their anger. I know what it's like to be around parents who bicker at each other, complain, shame and blame and eventually blow up with tears and tantrums. I learned to keep my head down to try to avoid it coming in my direction, suppressed my urge to bounce around, tried hard not to upset them and squashed my enthusiasm for life, and that became my normal behaviour.

Continuously being angry with other members of the family, when the anger is at their expense, will contribute to a child's depression, perhaps even cause it. Everyone else has to tiptoe around the 'angry one' and curtail their feelings and this leads to resentment. Chronic anger chokes out other feelings because there's no room for anyone else's feelings. An atmosphere of chronic anger promotes other angry exchanges such as sarcasm, cynicism, blame, vengeance etc. Then the 'angry one' may go into withdrawal, depression and loneliness and this leads to the 'don't bother them' period. It's a no-win situation for everyone.

How do you handle anger?

If you are patient in one moment of anger, you will escape a hundred days of sorrow.

Chinese proverb

Everyone has their own way of handling their own anger. Are you passive or are you explosive when you are angry? Anger is far too complex to unpack in a paragraph, suffice to say that positive anger is a natural emotion that is as healthy as happiness. There is nothing wrong with feeling angry and expressing it and, if we ignore our anger, it won't go away but fester inside us until we either explode or become depressed.

Anger that is not dealt with in childhood develops into depression as adults. It can also develop into abuse of self and others, which leads to mayhem. Behind every man and woman in jail for violent behaviour lies a part of them that is in deep pain. Childhood abuse creates abusive adults. Unexpressed anger can be very dangerous to both the individual and others. It is the anger that is suppressed that comes out as rage. We have to move on from our childhood rage in order to develop into competent and happy adults.

Many of us deny that we are angry but if we are depressed, then we have hidden anger. We are not encouraged to express our anger – especially as children and we are not taught how to release it. But unchecked anger leads us into situations we would choose not to be in. If we are angry and do not deal with it, it will land on the top of the angry heap inside us. It doesn't go away, it just accumulates.

Here is a checklist for hidden anger:

Chronic Pain in the neck or jaw
Sarcasm

Ironic humour
Boredom, apathy, disinterest, can't be bothered
Nightmares
Smiling when you don't want to
Controlling your voice
Grinding your teeth at night
Becoming irritated at irrelevant things
Body tics or spasmodic movements that you are unaware of
Stomach ulcers
Constant cheerfulness and 'grin and bear it' attitude
Refusing eye contact
Clenching a thumb in a fist
Over politeness
Not sleeping or sleeping too much
Frustration at everything around you
A feeling that life's not good enough

If you think you may have some unsettled anger but you don't recognise any of these signals in yourself, ask people close to you if they recognise any of them. Ask them how they can tell when you are upset about something. Just hear their response without sinking into a pit of 'contaminated shame'. Take it as good information. It is normal to deny that we are angry because it's the way our society is. When someone is angry others often look at him and say, 'Ooh, What's wrong with him?' It isn't generally accepted that releasing anger is a path to freedom. But it is. So, you must find yours. At this point you have to take it in blind faith that if you are depressed, you have repressed anger.

Take an hour aside for yourself and sit somewhere quiet and safe. Begin to write about what angers you. Make a list of at least ten things. You will start to see a common theme. Whatever your common theme is, allow yourself to indulge in the fury that accompanies your list. The ten things on your list will guide you towards your object of vehemence. Forget yourself as a nice polite person; see yourself as a screaming, childish, unreasonable toddler who's had enough.

If you need to take action to dispel the anger, thump the pillow, run it out, throw rocks in the sea, scream your head off or do something that satisfies the energy you feel. Let it all out and contain your fear that you will go out of control – you won't. Your mind will only release what you can deal with at that moment. Don't be afraid of your anger because it is very powerful. Use it for your good. Move it into determination, resolve and purpose. Make it work for you to bring about change but undertake this work away from the children – this is for adults only.

After you have done this you will feel more in control. You will feel a sense of calm and you may feel the pain that is buried beneath the anger. Anger and pain are on each end of a see-saw. If anger is pouring out then pain is buried deep. There is as much pain as there is anger. Enraged people are hurting badly. Letting out deep pain diffuses anger so it's important to stick with identifying what angers you and then finding out what hurt is sitting behind it. Don't worry, the pain will surface when you have made the room inside you and once you feel the pain and you are ready to release it, you can allow your tears to heal you.

Some of us possess a rage that is so fierce, we are scared to touch it. If you recognise this in yourself, it would be advisable to find a professional practitioner to assist you release the rage in a way that will not be harmful to you or anyone else. If you are aware that this rage sits inside you, you are halfway through taking care of yourself as awareness takes up half of the recovery from depression.

If you begin to release your buried anger and pain, you will unconsciously begin to help your depressed child. By respectfully getting help for yourself, you are teaching the child that it's OK to acknowledge difficult and painful feelings. This philosophy is central to helping a depressed child.

Where is the love?

You don't love a child because he is beautiful, but he is a beautiful child because you love him.

Anonymous

Does the love you have for your child come with conditions? What are those conditions? How did you choose them? What happens when the child doesn't meet the conditions?

These are profound questions and can raise some confusion amongst us. What we feel when we try to answer these questions largely depends on what we have received in our life. If we have never experienced what it is like to know that there is one person in the world who will love us no matter what we have done, said or thought, then we are deficient. The deficiency we have had depends on the amount of conditions our parents set us as children. If we have never experienced what it was like to be loved unconditionally then how can we give our children unconditional love?

The irony is that it is in the giving of unconditional love to a child that we can begin to establish what it may have felt like for those of us who didn't receive it. In loving unconditionally *we* gain a new freedom. This is the freedom to let go of rigid views about how children *should* be, the freedom to climb into the depths of our own gentleness and hand out some of that gentleness to a child regardless of what they have done, the freedom to trust that this letting go will not harm us but will help us to lean back in the armchair of life and relax.

If this feels too painful or you are dismissing these ideas, then maybe you are intolerant of your own humanness and fallibility. If you are angry at the very words 'unconditional love' perhaps you were denied as a child. Unconditional love is what we have a right to and if that wasn't given to you when you were a child it is still possible to claw something back. In seeking an adult who will help you through this difficult area and will offer you the sanctuary of unconditional regard, that they will hold the highest regard for you no matter what, then you have some chance to experience this complete acceptance of yourself. But it's not easy finding that person, that jewel in the crown of self-actualised human beings who have the capacity and wisdom to help you find the essence of yourself; but it is possible.

However, in acknowledging the purpose and prerequisite of unconditional love for the good of human happiness, it is possible to give it to yourself. There are many, many ways to do this – this is the central theme for so many spiritual courses, enlightened books, healing retreats, meditation programmes etc. The most profound way I have discovered has started with loving my children unconditionally and this has, paradoxically, helped *me* to feel utterly loved.

♉ THE CONTENTED FAMILY

Govern a family as you would cook a small fish – very gently.
Chinese proverb

What is a 'contented family'? Content means two things: **one** – satisfied with what one is or has; not wanting more or anything else, and **two** – power of containing; the holding capacity. A contented family is both of these things: the family is satisfied with what it has and is not wanting more; and the family holds and contains its members. A contented family is one to strive for. Here are some concepts that build a contented family.

A solid parental relationship

The qualities of the relationship between a mother and father, whether they are married or not will affect their children's emotional, intellectual and social wellbeing. It is generally believed that parents are the main source of support for each other and, as a result, the relationship that exists between them affects the couple's parenting skills. This in turn impacts on the adjustment of the children. For example, studies have shown that a contented relationship between parents promotes competence and maturity in their children. In contrast, relationship conflict may result in school difficulties and antisocial or withdrawn behaviour.[32]

Contented couples who are satisfied in their relationship are more likely to agree about expectations for their children and this gives the child consistency. Children also learn about attachment, security and loving behaviour, which will help them develop intimate relationships in adulthood.

Author Theodore Hesburge was quoted as saying, 'The best thing a father can do for his children is to love their mother.' How true because when a woman feels cherished by a man her self-esteem swells and she will, inadvertently, pass this onto her children. Consequently, when a man feels needed his esteem is augmented and he will invest it into his children.

---

32 Barbara H. Fiese and Karen A. Hooker, 'Family rituals in the early stages of parenthood', *Journal of Marriage and the Family*, 55: 3 (August 1993)

The roles are clearly defined

If there is anything we wish to change in the child, we should first examine it and see whether it is not something that could better be changed in ourselves.

Carl Gustav Jung, psychologist

Each family member has a role and each member knows what that role is and what is expected of them. Each member of the family will happily acknowledge their role. This will help a family function effectively.

For example, it is the parent's role to look after the children and provide for their needs. It is not the role of the adolescent to look after the younger children; it is the adolescent's responsibility to look after himself and become more independent and so prepare for the outside world. If the parents need help with the younger children, there will be a process of negotiation with the adolescent but the parents won't demand their help. If the parents are failing to be responsible for their roles then the extra work that other family members have to take on could leave them feeling resentful and overstretched.

Children are expected to take on some responsibility within the family and these roles will be allocated fairly and according to age. You may not expect a seven-year-old to cook the family meal but you could expect them to clear the dishes from the table. Likewise, you would ask an older child to cook a breakfast for the family as long as they have been taught how to do this. Contented families have members who take their roles seriously and do their best to fulfil their duties. This satisfaction promotes good relationships within the whole family.

But there will be flexibility. If there is a family crisis then these roles might change and each family member will be expected to pull their weight. As children grow older, these roles will change and adapt to the different age groups. Whereas the father may have been the one to keep the car clean, as the seventeen-year-old starts driving then he may take over that job.

Expression is valued

Do not train a child to learn by force or harshness; but direct them to it by what amuses their minds, so that you may be better able to discover with accuracy the peculiar bent of the genius of each.

Plato

A contented family values expression from each member. The governance of expression is understood: that it is trustworthy to express feelings, thoughts, desires and perceptions. A contented family allows freedom of speech and respects that everyone has different views and feelings. Expression of sorrow does not threaten anyone else, expression of anger can be heard and examined, a desire is acknowledged and thoughts are respected.

This freedom creates a safe place to share, which develops emotional awareness in every family member. Growing emotional awareness allows us to cultivate the capacity for recognising our own feelings and those of others, for motivating ourselves and for managing emotions in us and in our relationships. This means each family member has a self-awareness that enables them to recognise feelings and helps them manage their emotions. Children from a family that regularly expresses itself are better at handling relationships outside the family and this helps to increase their emotional health.

Healthy expression increases the capacity for emotional intimacy. It enhances the way people share with others without fear of rejection or abandonment and this allows them to be more honest about their true feelings.

Feedback for growth

It is not a bad thing that children should occasionally, and politely, put parents in their place.

Colette, writer

Honest feedback is the mirroring with empathy and evidence we talked about in 'Nurturing the Soul' in Chapter 3. Giving good feedback is an act of care and nurture. For children, this is where they gain their understanding of how they present themselves to others and if the feedback is offered in a clear and loving way, this will help them develop into whole, contented adults. For example, 'You seem angry. You are talking to me with a clenched jaw and I'm wondering what has happened to leave you feeling this way. Maybe I can help with whatever is troubling you.'

When talking about our own feelings, feedback is best given with 'I'. For example, 'I am feeling left out because you have been working on your car all day and I was hoping to spend some time with you.' The opposite feedback might be, 'You're always working on your car and you never spend any time with me.' The first sentence will elicit a more warm response even if they couldn't stop working on the car.

Parents are the models for children and the area of communication is one that children will copy. Starting sentences with 'You always…' or 'You never…' is not a warm approach. Starting sentences with 'I' offers the other person a way of opening up without recrimination.

With children it's important to allow them to express their desires no matter how unrealistic they are and to offer them balanced feedback so they get good perspective on their world and what is within acceptable limits. My seven-year-old son's Christmas list goes something like: one horse, one stable, shavings and hay, bridle and saddle, saddle soap, field for horse, computer and nothing else. He may get the soap but won't be receiving any of the others but we will enjoy his dream and contain his disappointment. If we stamp out his dream now he may learn it's no good expressing his desire and this will inhibit him in exploring other longings. When a more pragmatic (for the family budget) longing comes along, we shall encourage it and he will learn what the boundaries are. We want him to know he can reach for the sky.

We do what we say

Before I got married I had six theories about bringing up children; now I have six children and no theories.

John Wilmot, Earl of Rochester

Contented family members do what they say they will do. They show up when they say they will, they do house jobs as they said they would, they attend to others needs as they said they would. This shows trust and integrity. It builds respect for themselves and others. Children learn to rely on what is said to be accurate. They in turn will do as they say they will do.

Parents who do what they say they will do are self-disciplined – a wonderful tool for parenting. They are true to their word and children will also learn to be self-disciplined. Parents don't need to *promise* because their word is good enough. They don't say what they can't do, they don't promise things they can't achieve and they don't need affirmation of what they have done.

Conversely, parents who don't do what they say feel untrustworthy and unreliable. This model of behaviour leaves a child anxious about their needs getting met. Will Mum collect me on time? Will Dad give me the money for my schoolbooks? Children will believe that their parents didn't do what they said they would do because they (the child) didn't deserve it. Chronic anxiety leads to depression. Continually fulfilling responsibility leads to trust, self-reliance and confidence.

To do what we say we will do is about as good as it gets. There are hundreds of great parenting books yet in spite of all the good advice available, there are no rules. We have to try, fall flat on our face, brush ourselves down and try something else, but most of all accept our fallibility.

Fair fighting

The best way to keep children home is to make the home atmosphere pleasant – and let the air out of the tyres.

Dorothy Parker, writer

Conflict is normal. If there were no conflict in families you'd have to be concerned about the self-esteem of the family members because if there is no difference of opinion it will be a constrained environment. Conflict is necessary and healthy. It needs to be well managed for it to help enhance and strengthen relationships.

Fair fighting can reinforce relationships like nothing else. When it's carried out with an open and fair mind, fair fighting can help sweep out the flotsam and jetsam and allow the relationship to breathe in fresh air. Resolution with a win/win outcome leads to intimacy because there is nothing in between you. Intimacy is to stand on shared ground. It's the best place to help restore good emotional health and move depression out the way.

Here are the tools for fair fighting:

1. Stay in the moment. There is no point in going over all the things they have done in the past, just stick with the issue at hand.

2. Try not to overreact to difficult situations. By remaining calm it will be more likely that others will consider your viewpoint.

3. Be assertive, not aggressive. If you need a guide, start sentences with 'I' (assertive) and not 'You' (aggressive).

4. If you want honesty, be honest. There is no better tool to disarm a battle than honesty. Aim for accuracy rather than perfection or trying to get someone else to agree with you.

5. Express feelings in words, not actions. Actions can be abusive, avoid them.

6. Leave out the details. 'You were thirty minutes late.' 'No, I wasn't. I was only twenty minutes late.'

7. Be specific about what is bothering you. Vague complaints are hard to work on.

8. Don't blame. This will cause others to defend themselves. Instead, talk about how someone's actions affected you. Blame starts off with statements like, 'You always...' 'You never...' 'You should...' Instead start with, 'I felt ...' or 'The way you said that affected me like this...'

9. Mirror back what the other person has said and both agree on what you heard. This leaves little room for error.

10. Don't stomp off before the fight is finished. There is always a compromise when both parties get enough of a result to move forwards.

Being accountable with 'healthy shame'

Who is more foolish, the child afraid of the dark or the man afraid
of the light?

Maurice Freehill, writer

Being accountable is an old-fashioned idea that says you are
answerable for your actions – and inactions. If something
happens that is your responsibility you accept with grace.
Likewise, if something is omitted that shouldn't have been,
you concede with consideration. In a contented family,
accountability corresponds with love. Being accountable with
love is the opposite of the 'shame/blame' game.

It takes a certain wisdom to be accountable; when the
question comes up or something has gone wrong, it's you
who must absorb scrutiny. There's a subtle division between
'it's not finished' and 'I haven't finished it'. It's the *willingness*
to be accountable that matters. Being accountable for what
you do and what you fail or refuse to do is strength of
character.

In being accountable for the children of the family,
the parents will hold a certain amount of healthy shame.
Healthy shame is a healthy emotion that keeps us grounded
by providing us with limits. Healthy shame allows us to be
human, to make mistakes and ask for help. It also allows
us to see our own limits by preventing us wasting ourselves
on goals we can't reach, or on things we can't change.
By knowing our limits we can create a more spiritual
grounding because our energy will be integrated rather than
diffused.

When a child grows up with people who are emotionally
aware, the experience of shame that is passed on to the child
is healthy and nourishing. They know they can state their
needs without recrimination because they are human too.

Their parents will not be playing God but will be fair and firm. These confines will help the emotional wellbeing of a child to accept his own accountability, learning from his healthy shame.

An intimate family

Contented families have lots of fun. This fun is 'family intimacy' and this radiates throughout any family that is safe and warm. This intimacy encourages laughter, banter, playfulness and enjoyment. In what? In just *being*. Not 'having' or 'achieving', just *being* and *belonging*.

What is life but relationships? The rest is just stuff. When we, as parents, are gone, our children will not remember how much money we had in our bank account, which road we lived in or what car we drove but how much fun they had with us and how many great days we spent together and how much laughter took place and how nice it was to just hang out together.

It takes a minimum of twenty minutes a day to nurture the family intimacy. That's twenty minutes a day where everyone is all together and talking and this is easy to achieve over a meal. Time is the most important gift a parent can give a child.

Jason McQueen came from a wealthy background and when he was asked about growing up in this privileged home he said that one Christmas his father gave him the most precious gift he'd ever received. It was a small, lovely wrapped box and inside there was a note that said, 'Jason, this year I will give you 365 hours, an hour every day.' Jason explained that that present meant more to him than anything else he had received and his father kept his promise and renewed it every year. He said that he is the result of his father's time and intimacy. Being around families who share an intimacy is a delight.

An abundance of unconditional love

Unconditional love is the oxygen of the contented family. Unconditional love is what feeds all the members, ever reminding them that they are loved, supported and free to be themselves. This love goes beyond words; it's a spiritual essence that surrounds the family.

The heart of this life force is founded by the parents' belief that the children can have faith in their absolute devotion to them. They won't know but they will feel that no matter what they (the children) do, say, feel or think, their parents' love will never diminish. They are accepted, lock, stock and barrel by their parents and that belief is set in stone. That doesn't mean they will get away with things they shouldn't do or that they can manipulate that love to their own ends. Unconditional love means containment and fair discipline but with the wellbeing of the child as the central goal.

If you find this hard to swallow, may I suggest that you haven't experienced this feeling in yourself. No matter what age we are we can find this for ourselves. Yes, it doesn't come easy because we may not have built enough self-trust and self-reliance to depict ourselves to another. Paradoxically, if you show unconditional love to a child, you will receive it back from them. A child loves, no matter what, but for different reasons: a child needs to survive and will do what it can to keep his carers happy. Still, they offer their love and there is the gift for our taking.

The soul is healed by being with children.

Fyodor Dostoevsky, writer

★ THE FAMILY MEETING

The Family Meeting (FM) is an opportunity for all members of the family to get together on a regular basis. It is a gathering of the family in one place, at one time.

The idea for the FM came about while I was thinking about a better way for my new family to communicate since I had married for a second time. There was my seven-year-old son Gregory and Peter's two children, Sophie, seventeen and Joel, nineteen.

Having had a lot of experience in group work I knew that group work could be horrid if it wasn't well structured but it also could be incredibly profound if it was well managed. The times I spent in good groups gave me an amazing insight into the way others saw me and, from this personal work, I grew beyond my dreams and the benefits continue to emanate in every part of my life today. I knew that some of this experience could be put into place to help my new family gel and grow as one unit.

We have learned to talk to each other with openness, respect, love and humour. We have found ourselves helping each other out as a matter of course. Each family member is secure in the knowledge that the paths of communication are constantly open.

Since we began the FM, I have been asked into other families to help them to set up a regular FM to create a safe place to share and receive from other family members. The results have been staggering. Family members feel safe to disclose their real selves while feeling happy to confront an injustice. Spontaneous communication presides and everyone's fulfilment evolves.

It was a little daunting for us all to sit around the table and talk about how we were feeling. In fact, I found it quite uncomfortable the first few times, especially in talking to my young son on an equal basis without losing my role as a parent. It was a challenge and I had to be rigorous with myself as I realised that I often talked at him and not with him. However, as time went on it got easier. I sense that we now have a much more creative relationship, a priceless gift, and we spontaneously express ourselves.

We have now, as a family, developed the essence of our meeting to a few simple steps which can be followed by families anywhere. This simple structure has been put together to allow everyone to understand it. The whole concept is flexible to allow the ebb and flow of a family to preside.

How to run a Family Meeting

Hold a Family Meeting when you can – just make it fit in with your plans. This may mean you run a Family Meeting every morning before everyone disappears for the day; it may mean you hold one once a week, perhaps at the weekend when everyone is available. Children don't like to be left out of the Family Meeting so the schedule may well fit around them. The main thing is to make it fun and not a chore.

AGENDA
The agenda of the FM is as follows:

Open
1. What do we want to achieve today and what help do we need?
2. How is everyone feeling?
3. Any other business

Close
Agenda explained

Open
It's important to formally open the meeting.

What do we want to achieve today and what help do we need?
This is when everyone, one at a time, says what they would like to do today and asks for help from any other member to achieve it. They can ask other people for help or suggestions and that person can reply and then it moves on to the next person.

How is everyone feeling?
This is a chance for everyone to say how they feel, one at a time, starting with 'I feel'. No one comments or advises.

Any other business
Anyone can bring up any issues that don't fit into the other headings and this can be discussed by everyone.

Close
It's important to formally close the meeting.

The Golden Rules

1. Only one person talks at a time – there is no cross-talk as this violates safety. This is really, really important. Even if something is said that prompts extreme feelings in another person, the sanctity of the meeting means that there is no interruption, especially when people are expressing how they feel. This creates a safe and trusting place to share.
2. Everyone has a chance to speak and if they don't wish to speak, they 'pass' without anyone questioning why.
3. Talking goes around in a sequence so all members know when their turn is coming.
4. Members are not judged on their comments or statements.
5. Keep it short, anything from 5–20 minutes.

Who chairs?

The chair is taken by a different member of the family at each meeting. A rota is drawn up to establish the order of the chairperson.

Children from an early age must be included as chairperson – from about six or seven years old, maybe older, but it depends on the child. It is maybe helpful to a child if the format is simply written. Children love being included and it helps their self-esteem to be one of the team. Include them in chairing the meeting as soon as you can.

Expected outcomes:
- a family unity that has not been experienced before
- a growing sense of respect between all family members
- members feeling safer with other members

Children will gain:
- inclusion into the adult world
- a greater sense of autonomy
- an increasing self-respect
- a vehicle with which they can take some family responsibility
- an increase in their awareness of the world
- the ability to run a team meeting

Troubleshooting

A fractured meeting:
- the meeting may seem fractured at first, and people may want to leave the meeting; this is absolutely OK but the meeting will carry on without them and, once they leave, they cannot come back because this may distract everyone else.
- members can talk about their own feelings and how someone else may affect them; it is not good practice for

any member to tell another how they are. We must start
our comments with 'I'.

❁ this is not a chore – only fun.

A troubled meeting:

❁ if there are unresolved issues in the family then
the family meeting could become very painful and
confrontational and this would be especially prevalent if
there is a depressed child within the family.

❋ in this case, these matters can be addressed in or out of
the family meeting; it may mean that some extra help
is needed to get the family back on track. If the family
meeting does highlight some problems, then it has been
a valuable tool to establish the status quo so that healing
and wholeness may then take place.

Remember

❋ keep it simple, fun and animated – it is there as a
fantastic instrument to create harmony in the family

❁ a brilliant tool to bring together step-families

❋ if visitors are in the house, they are welcome to join the
meeting

❁ and embrace as a family at the end of the meeting doing
whatever feels comfortable

And finally

Please let me know the outcome of putting your Family
Meeting in place. I would be thrilled to hear what's
happened to your family and how it has helped a depressed
child because this is what the book is about.

Depression is a beginning, not an end, and if it is embraced
with compassion and wisdom, the whole family can heal and
grow with a profoundness that is impossible to imagine.

Resources

@ease
www.rethink.org/at-ease

Mental health resource for young people under stress or worried about their thoughts and feelings. Features information on causes of stress and practical advice on how to feel better.

ADFAM
www.adfam.org.uk

Adfam's vision is a United Kingdom where every family member facing problems with drugs or alcohol will have access to a range of specialised services.

Al-Anon Family Groups UK and Eire
www.al-anonuk.org.uk
London branch: 020 7403 0888 (or ring 020 7407 8180/7878 out of hours)
Glasgow branch: 0141 339 8884 (24 hours)

Understanding, support and information (including publications) and local groups for families and friends of people with alcohol problems, including young people affected by their parents' drinking.

Alateen
www.al-anonuk.org.uk/alateen.php
London branch: 020 7403 0888 (or ring 020 7407 8180/7878 out of hours)
Glasgow branch: 0141 339 8884 (24 hours)

Part of the Al-Anon fellowship for young people, aged 12 to 20, who are affected by a problem drinker. Members share ideas, experience and support, often in local groups. Alateen also produces support materials.

Alcohol Concern
www.alcoholconcern.org.uk

Alcohol Concern is the national agency for alcohol misuse. Website contains factsheets, publications, an online library database, news about what is happening in the alcohol field and links to useful websites.

Anorexia and Bulimia Care (ABC)
www.anorexiabulimiacare.co.uk

ABC is a national (within the UK) Christian charity working to support all those who suffer because of eating disorders and their associated problems.

Basement Project
www.basementproject.co.uk

A community resource providing support groups and helpful low-cost literature for individuals. Has a particular focus on abuse and self-harm.

BBC Parenting
www.bbc.co.uk/parenting

BBC Parenting provides information, support and expert help. The site is clearly divided into different age groups and offers information in small chunks for busy parents and practitioners.

BestTreatments
www.besttreatments.co.uk/btuk/conditions/35261.html
Telephone: 020 7383 6995

Guidance from the NHS on depression in children.

British Association for Counselling
www.bacp.co.uk
Tel: 0870 443 5252 (24 Hours)

Provides information on general counselling services (or ask your GP).

British Confederation of Psychotherapists
www.bcp.org.uk

National body linking mostly long-standing training and professional organisations in the field of psychoanalysis, analytical psychology, psychoanalytic psychotherapy and child psychotherapy.

Bullying Online
www.bullying.co.uk

Bullying Online was founded in 1999 by journalist Liz Carnel and her son John, as a direct result of their experience of dealing with school bullying. Help and advice for victims of bullying, their parents and school.

Change Our Minds
www.changeourminds.com

Produced by The Samaritans, the aim of this website is to prompt people to reconsider their attitudes towards emotional health. Includes information on stress, self-harm and teenage depression.

Childline
www.childline.org.uk
0800 1111

Free, 24-hour helpline service for children or young people in trouble or danger. Website also carries lots of information.

Children 1st

www.children1st.org.uk

Children 1st supports families under stress, protects children from harm and neglect and promotes children's rights and interests across Scotland.

Connexions

www.connexions-direct.com
080 800 13219 (free 8 a.m. to 2 a.m.)

Information, advice and support for 13- to 19-year-olds in England. Provides information on any relevant issue – including drugs, health and money. On the website, young people can web chat directly with a Personal Adviser, and there is also a freephone helpline. Local office details available on both helpline and website.

Depression Alliance

www.depressionalliance.org
0845 123 23 20

National network of self-help groups for people experiencing depression. Offers a quarterly newsletter, national pen friend scheme and correspondence service with advice, guidance, support and fellowship to people experiencing depression, and their carers. Produces booklets and leaflets on various aspects of depression.

Drug Concern

www.drug-concern.co.uk
(0845 120 3745 answerphone service out of hours)

Previously known as Parents For Prevention, this organisation provides a helpline, support groups and training for parents and carers concerned about their child's drug use.

Drugscope
www.drugscope.org.uk

In-depth information on all aspects of drug use, with frequently asked questions about drugs in the 'Drug Information' section.

Eating Disorders Association (EDA)
Website: www.edauk.com
Adult Helpline: 0845 634 1414
Youth Helpline: 0845 634 7650

Information and help on all aspects of eating disorders including anorexia nervosa, bulimia nervosa and binge eating disorder.

Eating Disorders Research Unit
Institute of Psychiatry, King's College London
www.iop.kcl.ac.uk/IoP/Departments/PsychMed/EDU/index.shtml

The aim of this website is to ensure that knowledge about eating disorders from research and clinical centres is available to all those with an interest in eating disorders, whether they have personal experience of an eating disorder, are a friend or relative of someone who does or are a health professional.

Families Anonymous (FA)
www.famanon.org.uk
0845 1200 660

A worldwide fellowship of relatives and friends of people involved in the abuse of mind-altering substances, or with related behavioural problems. Many local groups across the UK.

Familyrapp
www.familyrapp.com

A website designed to answer many different parenting questions in a single site. Includes a drugs section and discussion boards.

Frank
www.talktofrank.com
0800 77 66 00

The website has a section especially for parents to provide you help and information to talk to your children about drugs including: useful tips on how to manage those tricky teenage conversations; how to identify different drugs and the effects they can have; details of organisations offering practical help and support in your area.

Gingerbread
www.gingerbread.org.uk
0800 018 4318

Gingerbread offers a phone advice service for lone parents. Also provides day-to-day support for lone parents and their children through local self-help groups.

Healthy Place Depression Community
www.healthyplace.com/Communities/Depression/children.asp

A community site helping those with depression and depressed children.

Kids Company
www.kidsco.org.uk

Provides emotional, practical and educational support to profoundly vulnerable young people.

Kidscape
www.kidscape.org.uk
08451 205 204

The helpline is for the use of parents, guardians or concerned relatives and friends of bullied children.

Lifeline
www.lifeline.org.uk

This organisation provides leaflets on Drug Myths and Drug Facts for parents, plus parents' leaflets on the South Asian Community and Drugs (in Urdu/English and Bengali/English).

Mental Health Foundation
www.mentalhealth.org.uk
020 7803 1101

Leading UK charity that provides information, carries out research, campaigns and works to improve services for anyone affected by mental health problems, whatever their age and wherever they live.

Mind
www.mind.org.uk
0845 766 0163

Works to support those experiencing mental distress. The website provides a range of information through factsheets and booklets, as well as details of local Mind associations.

National Association for Children of Alcoholics
www.nacoa.org.uk
0800 358 3456

NACOA provides information, advice and support to children of alcoholics through its free, confidential helpline.

National Association of Citizens Advice Bureaux
www.citizensadvice.org.uk
020 7833 2181

Offices nationwide providing free, impartial and confidential
advice and help.

National Family & Parenting Institute
www.familyandparenting.org
020 7424 3460

Independent charity working to support parents in bringing
up their children, to promote the wellbeing of families and
to make society more family friendly.

National Family Mediation
www.nfm.u-net.com
020 7485 8809

Can provide information on local mediation services for
families around family break up, divorce and separation.

National Self-Harm Network
www.nshn.co.uk

Campaigns for a better understanding of self-harm and
provides a free information pack. Contact NSHN if you are
worried because you self-harm or you are close to someone
who does.

NSPCC
www.nspcc.org.uk
0808 800 5000

Advice and information for adults and young people on any
issue of concer.

Parentline Plus
www.parentlineplus.org.uk
0808 800 2222

Support to anyone parenting a child – the child's parents, stepparents, grandparents and foster parents. Runs a freephone helpline, courses for parents, develops projects and provides a range of information.

Parents Against Drug Abuse (PADA)
www.pada.org.uk
08457 023 867

An organisation set up to support parents of drug users. A large percentage of helpline workers have experienced drug use within their own families.

ParentsCentre
www.parentscentre.gov.uk

Information and support for parents on how to help with your child's learning, including advice on choosing a school and finding childcare.

Project SPEAR
www.projectspear.com

This website has been produced to encourage and support those who are struggling with personal issues including self-injury. Support materials, personal stories, advice and experience are offered for those who want help, and for those who want to help others.

Radio 1 One Life
www.bbc.co.uk/radio1/onelife

Information on a range of subjects – from education to travel and health issues. It has a detailed drugs and alcohol section, with Q&A sections and real life stories. It is aimed at young people in Radio One target age range.

Release

www.release.org.uk
020 7729 5255

Provides a range of services dedicated to meeting the health, welfare and legal needs of drug users and those who live and work with them. Has recently launched a support and information service for heroin users and people who care for them.

Rethink

www.rethink.org
020 8974 6814

Runs a helpline for people with schizophrenia and their families.

Royal College of Psychiatrists

www.rcpsych.ac.uk

Offer a range of leaflets on childhood depression including books you can download from the website.

Samaritans

www.samaritans.org.uk
08457 90 90 90

The Samaritans exists to provide confidential emotional support to any person, irrespective of race, creed, age or status who is in emotional distress or at risk of suicide; 24 hours a day. Can be contacted by e-mail, telephone, writing, or by visiting one of over 200 local branches (details are on the website).

Saneline

www.sane.org.uk
0845 767 8000

A helpline for people coping with mental illness and provides information about local support services.

SIARI

www.siari.co.uk

Extensive UK resource offering information and support to people who self-harm and their carers. Features self-injury research and references, book lists, poems, artwork, stories, message boards, access to an online support group for helpers and a section for counsellors.

The Anna Freud Centre

www.annafreudcentre.org
020 7794 2313

Helps children and families with behavioural and emotional problems.

The Blenheim Project

www.theblenheimproject.org
020 8960 5599

Drug service that produces a range of leaflets including 'How to Stop' for opiate users and 'How to Help' for families of drug users.

The Hideout

www.thehideout.org.uk

A website that helps children who are living with domestic abuse.

The National Treatment Agency
www.nta.nhs.uk

The National Treatment Agency (NTA) is a special health authority, created by the government in 2001 to improve the availability, capacity and effectiveness of treatment for drug misuse in England. In other words, to ensure that there is more treatment, better treatment and fairer treatment available to all those who need it.

The Site
www.thesite.org

A 'guide to the real world' for young people aged 16–25 with accessible info and advice on drugs, health, sex and relationships, plus in-depth features on clubbing, festivals, holidays and student life. Well-used discussion boards.

Turning Point
www.turning-point.co.uk

Works with individuals and their communities in the areas of drug and alcohol misuse, mental health and learning disabilities. Has particular expertise in working with people who have complex needs and are facing multiple social challenges. Its site provides details of the local projects and services it provides.

UK Parents
www.ukparents.co.uk

A magazine site for parents. Includes discussion boards and problem pages for information on depressed children.

Wrecked

www.wrecked.co.uk

This NHS site is aimed at teenagers and provides basic information and facts about alcohol use, including true stories and a quiz.

YoungMinds

www.youngminds.org.uk
0800 018 2138

Provides help for parents concerned about a young person's mental health. The service offers a variety of leaflets and booklets, including one that explores how divorce and separation affect children and young people.

Young People and Self-Harm

www.selfharm.org.uk

This website provides information on a wide range of activities and initiatives that relate to young people and self-harm. Includes details of useful contacts and publications.

Youth Access

www.youthaccess.org.uk
020 8772 99001

A national membership organisation for youth information, advice and counselling agencies. Provides details of and referrals to local youth agencies and counselling services for young people aged between 14 and 25, but does not offer direct advice.

Index